WEALTH CREATION

THE SPEED

Changing The Speed of Wealth Creation is far more important than generating an income!!!

Rob Wilson

(Wealth Creation - The Speed)
Copyright © 2023 by (Wealth Accumulation Concepts)

ISBN 978-0-9721065-9-7

Printed in USA

Dedication

These series of Wealth Creation is dedicated to the many families that I have comes across in my work. It is also dedicated to you the now reader, whether you are reading just this book or the entire series, I am in prayer that you experience wealth creation personally.

I especially wish that you who have chosen to read this series find what they are seeking.

To: Pastor Allen

Rob Wilson   5/21/22

FAST MONEY

Your decision to trust the wealth creation process and the effect of time on investing is powerful!

Table of Contents

Foreword

Rob Wilson has captured the essence of being prepared for financial success. Understanding the financial opportunities and barriers are the first steps to becoming equipped to create wealth that will ultimately change the speed. Being a winner in the financial arena takes action.

Rob understands that you will not always get it right but strategically thinking about savings, investing, and building a strategy will be instrumental in living the life you most desire.

Rob is the master of creating the financial roadmap to do this in an effective and efficient manner. His extraordinary way of explaining the terms and potential outcomes when you understand your capacity to succeed will most definitely lead to generating wealth.

With the influence of Fintech, making decisions about money moves must be pre-planned. Rob explains in no uncertain terms, that the "Speed of wealth creation is far more important than creating income".

His ingenious way of walking you step by step through the wealth creation process levels the playing field that will, for sure, close the great wealth divide.

A great testament to Rob's commitment to your success is that he does not sugarcoat the requirements necessary to build your wealth. You must hold yourself accountable, learn ways to diversify your assets, keep good records of your success and failures. And, you must do this consistently!

Time management concerning your financial affairs begins now. Becoming part of the wealth generating regime is not easy nor should it be. Rob effectively provides examples that instruct you how to calculate wealth building through progressive investments.

More importantly, he illustrates that you do not have to have a lot of money to start. Knowledge is power. Commitment, desire, and effort are the things you need to make decisions quickly for your financial well-being.

I am extremely happy that Rob Wilson has taken the time to share his gift of helping everyone succeed in their quest to build wealth.

Sheilah Montgomery, Proactive Impact, LLC CEO, CCE, I-CUDE

Preface

I am about to take you on a journey, one that if I get this right will not only change your life, but that of the next three generations. This is huge for me because I have been right where you are or even lesser than most of you as you start off.

I started from homelessness, I started from financial distress! Some of you may be currently dealing with financial distress and not really understand it for what it is and how it is the weight that holds you down.

Financial distress is a condition in which you cannot generate sufficient income, making it unable to meet or pay your financial obligations. This is generally due to poor budgeting, overspending, too high of a debt load, lawsuit, or loss of employment.

Sadly to say, the signs of financial distress are ignored and get out of control fast and can be devastating. There may come a time when severe financial distress can no longer be remedied because your obligations have grown too high and cannot be repaid. This is why bankruptcy has been the only option for many.

It is hard to experience financial distress and be in a situation where your debt costs are much more than your monthly income. These obligations as basic include items such as your home or rent payments, car payments, credit cards, and utility bills.

As I have explained in this series, situations like these tend to extend the period of time and may ultimately force you to relinquish assets secured by their debts and lose your home or car, or face eviction.

If you are not in financial distress, you may be in that other space of believing that when you make a lot of money, that means you are rich. What does rich mean? Oops! I believe this might be the first time that I mention richness in this entire series.

Listen, the assumption is that having a great deal of money or assets makes you rich. But let's think about that for a minute.

How are you spending your money? Just because you may be making a large amount of money doesn't necessarily mean you are rich.

This is a common trap of high-income earners, although they may be bringing in a lot of money, they are also spending a lot of money.

There is this idea that they need to show off their money and enjoy their money, which often leads to overspending. Someone who I admired made a quote that has helped me help others. James E. Young, former President and CEO of Citizens Trust Bank stated "Your Salary is not Your Wealth"

You must realize that instead of spending your money as it comes in, you can start your money working for you through investments, then earning passive income on those investments. When you get your money working for you and have your money generating even more money, this is the sweet spot.

Taking a look at your net worth is the best way to measure where you are financially. It is called your net worth = all of your assets (what you own) less all of your liabilities (what you owe).

The higher your net worth number is, the richer you are. Your wealth lies in the assets you own, such as investments, assets such as rental properties, and anything you own that holds value for a long time.

Your net worth lies in your behavior with and around money. How you spend, save, and manage your money will determine how wealthy you are or will become.

One of the common threads between the most affluent people is that they are not showy about it. They have incredible amounts of money but are not commonly seen vacationing on the most expensive yachts, wearing flashy clothes, or living an excessive lifestyle.

A key layer of your mindset is the ability to plan, schedule and prioritize, and I've seen many rich people lose the strategy at this stage.

I do not want you burning entire days working on things that don't really matter in the long run. Do not get trapped feeling like you have made progress, but all that you have done is just spinning your wheels.

As a wealth creator you know to focus relentlessly on what matters. Hey you might only accomplish a single thing one day, but it's the thing that tilts the scale to success.

If you want to improve your prioritizing layer, scrutinize your to-do list carefully. What item or items on that list have the power to make you grow?

Congratulations—you've found your priority. Focus as much of your energy on that as possible. This may mean automating or delegating everything else.

Remember long-term investing is the only strategy that can help you become rich from nothing. Oops! I said it! A buying and selling investment asset frequently is not only more expensive, it is less profitable. The longer you stay in the market, the less the risk of losing your money and the more returns you will have.

For example, a study of the S&P 500 between 1926 and 2019 has shown that the longer you stay in the market, the more likely you are to make money.

If you stay for five years, the chance of losing money is 5%, whereas if you stay invested in the market for 10 years, it decreases significantly – to just 0.2%.

Changing the Speed

Introduction

Yes I want you to change the speed of wealth creation. It will be required of you to think fast, decide fast, act fast and move on fast.

It means that you need to have more than tactical skills for change, and, more than a long range strategy for impact. It means you have to be prepared to be the person who can be the creator of wealth for your family.

This means that you have to simplify your lives, become clearer about who you are, who you are not, and what you want as you build your generational wealth. Imagine this.

You start investing. You have never been at this level of investing before. There's nothing immediately intimidating to you about investing. Yet, you have to deal with financial situations that once crushed you.

You are not thinking about quitting. You are thinking about how you can convert this opportunity so you can make a difference on your journey. Making the decision to create wealth is essential to change the generations coming behind you.

The idea that you want to cross a bridge and enter through a door that a very few people will travel to is in itself the most powerful thought you can have at this time. This series of books on wealth creation is not much different than other books on money.

What I believe I am doing is equipping people like you with new tools and processes in approaching wealth creation. There are many things that have popped up since 2020 as a fast track to riches.

There are financial books that are motivating and full of inspiration, yet they do not direct you to a process that generates real wealth creation.

Since I am talking about the speed to wealth creation, there will be things that I will not talk about. For instance, just about everyone talks about rule of 72 as being the best process of identifying just how long it would take to double your money.

Below you will see what Rule 72 can impact your investment.

1. The Rule of 72 is a simplified formula that calculates how long it'll take for an investment to double in value, based on its rate of return.

2. The Rule of 72 applies to compounded interest rates and is reasonably accurate for interest rates that fall in the range of 6% and 10%.

3. The Rule of 72 can be applied to anything that increases exponentially, such as GDP or inflation; it can also indicate the long-term effect of annual fees on an investment's growth.

4. This estimation tool can also be used to estimate the rate of return needed for an investment to double given an investment period.

For different situations, it's often better to use the Rule of 69, Rule of 70, or Rule of 73.

How this works is simple, you take whatever the interest rate of your investment and divide it by the number 72 and you will have your time period of doubling your investment. You have a fixed interest rate of 6% on a 1000.00 investment, you now divide $72/6 = 12$years.

Twelve years to double your money is not speed in my opinion. I can think of several ways to double your money much quicker. The process that you are about to read and learn is going to require change.

As you encounter the change, you need to move more quickly than you have in the past. You will find when you do, that much of what you are now doing is adapting to changing circumstances. The quicker you do so, the better off you will be.

It may seem like I am suggesting you acquire a new set of skills. In order for those situational skills to work for you, you need a change in your own sense of who you are.

If in every new situation that you encounter you feel the need to accommodate yourselves to the tribal rituals of the crowd, then you will never find yourselves in a position of creating wealth.

The greatest change you go through is in your own self-awareness. Without growth here, there is little chance of growth as a creator of wealth. The faster you change, the faster you'll discover a life of impact. It is that simple.

It's tempting to keep up with the Joneses and spend money on gadgets, luxury items that do not hold value, and "stuff" that you don't need.

But if you are spending more money than you are making, that accumulates debt, and debt costs money to carry. Your money would better serve you invested where it pays a return.

When you invest your money and are earning interest on top of interest, your money grows at an exponential rate. However, the reverse is true when you are carrying debt. You pay money to have that debt at an exponential rate as well, and it eats up your money quickly.

Having a plan is by far the most important secret of all. A goal without a plan is just a wish, so for you to achieve your financial goals, you need to plan out your investments.

When you plan and map out your goals, it's easier to measure your results against your goals and hold yourself accountable. Having a plan makes your goals actionable.

And yet, the vast majority of people never build any serious wealth. Rather than creating wealth over time, they just stay afloat decade after decade, moving through life spending as much as they make.

At most, they build a small nest egg, and rely on the government or a pension to support them in retirement.

The bottom line is if you are not giving your financial plan the attention that it needs to build your wealth, it is time to do so.

The return on that investment of time, money and energy will multiply itself over the years and will likely be the best investment you have ever made for yourself and your financial future.

Remember don't be too conservative, although being too speculative is a sure-fire way to risk all the savings you have worked for, being too conservative can be equally damaging in terms of limiting your wealth.

Taking some risks in your financial life — from investing a bit more aggressively to starting your own business — is a necessary component if you want to generate outsized levels of wealth.

If you put all of your money into Treasury bills, for example, you'll actually generate a negative real return after taking taxes and inflation into account.

Owning some stocks, real estate, your own business or even some crypto currency are ways to gain exposure to higher potential returns on your investments. Just understand that while speculation has a role in generating wealth, it also brings additional risk to the table.

You are investing in yourself NOW and learning how to manage your money and the return on this investment will be immeasurable, provided that you implement what you've learned.

There will be a high return on investment for years to come when you use the financial skills you have learned from this series.

The Speed

Chapter One

You Heard This Before!

In this chapter, I am going to talk about that one thing that is on the top of your mind: wealth creation. There are a lot of books and stories that talk about the mindset, saving and investing and wealth. I am going to talk about them all before I give you my strategies for changing the speed.

First, let's look at money – Money is what makes the world go 'round. The bible teaches money answereth all things.

And it's also what stresses a lot of us out. It is a fact that you are more likely to worry about your financial situation than anything else – whether it's the amount of debt you are carrying, not having money set aside for unexpected expenses, or not having enough to retire. Money oh Money...

Here is the thing, even when you feel financially comfortable – you have enough money to meet your needs, pay your bills, save for the future and even accumulate wealth, one thing remains true: having more money doesn't eliminate challenges.

When you say that money is what you want, what are you really saying? The truth is that you want freedom, security, and a certain lifestyle, opportunities for your families, the ability to contribute and any number of other things.

You Heard This Before

What you may want could be based on the number of active years you have left. You are limited by the number of years you have to be able to run around actively. A twenty-year-old today probably has another 20–30 years of active working life left.

This is to say, as you age, the physical labor you can offer reduces. This is the period when you can set the foundation of your wealth.

The moment you have decided to create your wealth then you should take action towards making it happen by starting a dedicated savings account. Irrespective of the amount you decide to save periodically, your savings should be automated to make it easier to achieve discipline and consistency. You should also invest your money in opportunities that I will discuss more later.

Of course when picking a savings account, it is important to find one with zero or minimal fees and with considerable returns. Your saved-up cash should not just sit in a bank, it should work for you to generate returns. This is how you grow wealth, steadily.

There's no right or wrong and it's different for everyone. Ultimately, creating wealth is about what gives you abundance. Learning how to create wealth means defining what life on your terms looks like and putting a plan in place to make it happen.

Once you shift your mindset to realize that money is just a vehicle, not the end goal, you can take massive action to grow wealth and improve. It's important to consider the meaning of wealth as you build it, so you can focus on making progress.

While there is no one rule for wealth creation, to build wealth one must follow a certain level of discipline. Here are the three secret disciplines you need to master to grow your wealth.

This chapter is titled "You have seen this before" because you have. The things I am going to share here are things you have heard a hundred times. I will share with you things that experts say are the secrets to wealth creation, when in fact they are things that are unlikely to impact the poor.

Please do get offended by clearly identifying the poor. If you look around you, you'll probably notice that you are surrounded by so many things aimed at making you spend money on things you do not need.

If you have a goal of becoming wealthy someday, you should learn to postpone buying until you have enough. This is not to say you shouldn't enjoy some of life's little luxuries. The point here is that you could always delay buying luxuries until you achieve your important money goals. You should learn to live way below your income.

Or better, ask these questions: Do I need this item to survive? Does this item bring me additional cash? Am I buying this to impress my friends?

Do not get caught with the Joneses, they are all around you. They are those families and friends who spend money just to impress others.

Just consider your neighbors with all the flashy toys, your friends who buy the latest gadgets to show off but are barely able to pay their rent.

It does not take much to be like the Joneses – all you need is to spend your little savings on what the Joneses are

3

buying. This never-ending race to be like the Joneses always leads you to make poor financial decisions that are detrimental to wealth building.

This is not a new concept, you have heard this before, and the poor are always taught subprime information about business and wealth creation. Wait, I may need to reexamine my own approach with this process.

Maybe sub-prime is not the correct way to describe this, the information is factual, and it is just very vague. An example of what is taught about the fastest way to build wealth is to spend less than you earn. Live below your means. Save the remaining and invest where it grows steadily over time.

That is how you build wealth fast. However, many people never really build wealth as they keep spending as much as they earn. Then, later in life, they depend on a pension or their children to support them in retirement.

How do you create wealth from nothing? I am asked this question over and over and in the past I would make recommendations by simply pulling something up on Google and sharing it as the authority. Here are the things commonly given.

Educate yourself. Understand how to build wealth.

Liquidate assets you don't need anymore.
Avoid unnecessary debts and wasteful spending.
Automate your savings
Invest
Share your financial knowledge with your circle. What is better than one wealthy person? Wealthy people.
I just want to ask you how that workout for you?

Listen there is no shortage of get-rich-quick schemes, from the latest crypto coin to flipping penny stocks. Don't be fooled by their promises of easy wealth—schemes hide giant risks and the vast majority of investors end up losing money.

Instead, I want you to spend your time learning how to build wealth, which requires you to make an investing plan and adopt a long-term mindset. After this chapter I will be talking about creating that investment plan and the process to becoming a wealth creator.

In the meantime, I am going to give you eight simple steps to get started building sustainable wealth as you learn these steps. Keep in mind that you may be learning principles and applications that seem too simple. Trust the process.

Start by Making a Plan

Building wealth starts with making a financial plan. That means taking the time to identify your goals and game out how you can accomplish them. Building wealth begins with a vision and a plan that is connected to your purpose.

It's recommended that you start off by hiring a financial advisor is a great way to begin making your plan for building wealth. It's a more expensive option, particularly for those who are just starting out, but choosing an advisor who's a certified financial planner (CFP) means you're paying for planning experience. Do not allow this statement to detour you.

I am creating a process here that just might get you going at a faster pace than you've been on in creating a plan. By now if you have read the other books of the series you are well on your way. If by chance you are diving in this book first, then pay close attention to details.

You Heard This Before

Make a Budget and Stick to It

I have been teaching personal finance and money management for over twenty five years. My biggest challenge has always been trying to get people to understand the power of budgeting. Plenty of people dread the "B" word, but budgeting is a key plank in your wealth building strategy.

Building a budget and sticking to it helps increase your chances of carrying out your plan and achieving your financial goals. Budgets also help you understand where your money goes each month and prevent behaviors that can endanger your goals, like overspending.

Let this sink into your head and your heart, every single process or entity that you encounter has some form of a budget. It is the key element that allows them to forecast their salary and profits. Losers are the ones who determine that they can operate without a budget.

Build Your Emergency Fund

Oh how I hate how this statement right here has been used and is setting people up to fail. Building your emergency fund is taught by many to have 3 – 6 months of expenses saved for emergencies.

Things like when the furnace goes out or the refrigerator quits working, you don't have to worry where the money comes from if you have emergency savings.

In most cases your credit cards bear the brunt of any emergencies and cause you to incur extra costs and fees, like sky-high interest rates. Yes, by building an emergency fund, you can protect your credit as well as reap the benefits of earning interest on an online savings account—all the while enjoying the

6

peace of mind of knowing you have money in the bank to cover life's surprises.

My issue with the title (Build Your Emergency Fund) is simply to put people in the mindset of it being enough when unexpected things happen. So consider this, things will happen, in addition to the water heater and refrigerator there is loss of work and income, there is divorce and sickness.

Oftentimes 3-6 months' income is not enough. It was back in the 70's and 80's, it is not enough in 2023 and beyond. There is a new standard of requirements for savings in my opinion. If starting a campaign with 3-6 months of saving helps you to get started, by all means do so. Just don't get stuck there.

Remember, these are the traditional things that are taught for you to create wealth. I am not trying to diminish its value to the process. I am making you aware that it is not enough. These tools and processes will elevate you from your current financial position. I actually love this next one, automate!

Automate Your Financial Life

There can be danger in just about anything, never getting too comfortable with anything. However, by making saving, investing and bill pay automatic, you all but eliminate the chance that you will forget to set aside money for your goals or make progress on paying off your debts.

I believe that it is important you have the aggregate amount you've budgeted for each of your expenses and goals automatically deducted from your account and applied to each expense.

This can become especially valuable when it comes to saving and investing. It helps you to resist the temptation to spend rather than invest. Soon, you won't miss the money that is being automatically deducted and your contributions will be made on a regular basis.

There is great power here. You can be freed (at least somewhat) from investing your energies in such thoughts and worries. By simply automating your finances it can not only be a smart money move, it will save you on late fees, it may also help alleviate some of the stress surrounding payment deadlines.

Many of the benefits of automation include helping avoid fees, sticking to your monthly budget, and enjoying peace of mind, plain and simple!

Figuring out where to start (or whether) to automate personal finances might seem like a lot of work up front, but it can help boost your financial success. And it's actually quite simple once you dive in.

Pay Down Debt!

The one step that I know people find challenging is dealing with debt. Of course, not all debt is created equal—and some, like mortgages, may even be considered "good" debt, thanks to their general low interest rates and wealth building potential.

Some experts even think of a mortgage payoff as a type of forced savings account because you'll likely see at least a portion of your monthly payment back when you sell.

But if you're rolling over a lot of bad debt, like high-interest credit card bills, every month, you may jeopardize your financial goals.

8

That's why it's important to have a plan for your repayment, with the ultimate goal of having a debt-free life. As your balances fall, you'll have even more money to put towards your emergency savings and investments.

Max out Your Retirement Savings

I know you have heard these before. LOL! This is what I am trying or hoping to get you to see, your wealth creation is not going to happen with the following.

Yes Uncle Sam gives you a few different ways to save up for retirement, and experts encourage you to take advantage of as many as you can. That means putting the most you can toward your employer's retirement plan—think 401(k)—as well as individual retirement accounts (IRAs).

If contributing the legal maximum is going to be a stretch for you right now, make sure you're at least saving enough to get any 401(k) match your company provides. That means if your employer offers a 3% match, you're contributing at least 3% of your salary each pay period.

Don't get discouraged if you can't invest a lot to begin with. Most of my clients invested a small amount of money for a long period of time. The power of compounding, then, helps turn these invested small sums into fortunes.

Stay Diversified

If you're clinging to the idea that people only become wealthy by having highly concentrated positions—perhaps by holding large amounts of Bit coin—consider loosening your grip.

You Heard This Before

Having a diversified portfolio with different types of investments can both protect the wealth you've accumulated and position you to reap rewards even in market downturns.

I will be showing you a way to build your financial portfolio and referencing you back to the book titled "The Mindset" as we also change the speed of wealth creation for you.

A diversified portfolio includes a mix of assets that do not necessarily move in the same direction and in the same magnitude at all times and is designed to help reduce volatility over time.

Up Your Earnings

This is another one of those that you hear all the time. The more you earn over your lifetime, the more money you have available to invest. While it isn't a move that you can make at any time, investing in yourself by raising your income is an important step when it comes to how to build wealth.

If you've been living comfortably on your current salary and you receive an increase, this is the perfect opportunity to begin the path to building wealth.

Whether that means contributing more toward your retirement savings, paying down debt or bumping up your emergency fund savings I would recommend you save at least half of every raise you get to position yourself for a secure retirement.

This allows you to improve your quality of life gradually while also ensuring you don't fall victim to standards of living that will be impossible for you to maintain in retirement.

Listen, with goals like retirement and generational wealth creation, the stock market is and will be your friend. It can be positively terrifying when the market tanks. And it will tank — it always does.

But it always goes back up, too. If I can get you investing in a diversified portfolio — and of course you will! — Then you will be investing in thousands of companies in the U.S. and abroad.

Rationally, you can agree that while many businesses do fail, many others thrive, and new companies are constantly emerging. When the market is tanking, it's no surprise that plenty of investors find themselves thinking this: "Well, I'll just get out of the stock market now, and get back in later, when things are looking up."

Trouble is, it's impossible to know when the market's going to turn around. And by exiting the market, even for a short time, you risk missing out on all kinds of gains.

So the next time the market falls, try this mantra on for size instead: This is the best sale ever, and you don't even have to get up off the couch or click away from [whatever show you're currently binge-watching].

Thanks to those periodic transfers I'm making from my paycheck to my retirement accounts, I'm currently buying new mutual fund shares at a fraction of what they cost during the market's high point.

When the market does turn around, as you know it will, you are going to own way more shares than before, and they're all going to rise in value."

You Heard This Before

Remember, wealth isn't usually built overnight, it takes time and consistency. This is especially true if your goal is to build generational wealth, which is when you pass assets down to future generations.

You don't need tons of money to start building wealth, so even if you don't have much to start with, you can start where you are.

The more you contribute towards saving and investing and the sooner you start, the faster you should build wealth. Also, don't be discouraged if you're just starting out, as long as you stick with it, compound interest will eventually work its magic.

Get ready to change the speed!

Chapter Two

Implementation

Some may question why I would discuss implementation so early in the book. I am okay with that, after all I want you to experience wealth creation in a realistic way for you and your family. You have heard much of this information before and yet you are still in search of wealth creation.

What I hope you gain from this chapter are the tools and direction you will need to create generational wealth. Again, this is about having knowledge and understanding about creating wealth and planning every phase of it.

Implementation for you simply means carrying out the activities necessary to work your plan. Executing your plan can and will be a very complex mission, as it requires the coordination of a wide range of activities, the overseeing of the household mission, the management of your assets, among other issues.

Consider your implementation plan—also known as a strategic plan— as the outlines and the steps you should take when accomplishing your investment goals.

This plan will combine strategy, process, and action and will include all parts of the project from scope to budget and beyond.

Put It In Action

I will guide you as I discuss what an implementation plan is and how to create one.

Wealth creation requires planning to be successful. Would you build a house without a blueprint? Probably not, because nailing pieces of wood together without a plan could lead to disaster.

The same concept is true in your financial world. An implementation plan functions as the blueprint to help you reach your desired goals. Your plan should include everything from the budget, to the invest strategy, to the assets allocation.

Your implementation plan becomes your document that outlines the steps you and your family should take to accomplish the set goals. Implementation planning is the counterpart to a strategic plan.

If the strategic plan details what strategies you will use to hit a specific goal, the implementation plan is the step-by-step guide for how those goals will be achieved.

Have a committed purpose for your implementation plan to ensure that you and the household can answer the "who", "what", "when", "how", and "why" of your wealth creation before moving into the execution phase. In simple terms, it's the action plan that turns your strategy into specific tasks.

I know that you may find it difficult to share your desire with others. However I do believe highly in understanding that you can't do the process alone. You should have an accountability partner. You are going to need a good way to know whether your implementation plan is effective by handing it to someone inside of your circle to see if they can understand the plan in its entirety. Your implementation plan should leave no questions unanswered.

You must want your implementation plan to be comprehensive and beneficial, so you will need to follow specific steps and include the right components. I am going to create steps for you as you start creating your plan to reduce the risk of gaps in your strategy.

The first step in your implementation process is defining your goals. Why are you wishing to create wealth? You need to determine what you hope to accomplish when your goals are complete, like whether you hope to build cash flow or reinvestment strategy. Starting with your objectives in mind can help flesh out your plan.

Later in the book I will look to provide you with elements to help you define your goals, you and your household may want to ask questions about your goals such as, "What are you trying to achieve with this mission of wealth creation? What deliverables do you hope to produce?

It is okay to brainstorm risk scenarios, although you will perform a more in-depth risk assessment later on in your implementation plan, brainstorming potential risk scenarios early on gives you a more realistic idea of what you're able to achieve.

15

Put It In Action

I have learned in my practice that many of many clients feel that looking at a potential risk will only bring them into play. Risk is real, please say it again and now repeat it over and over risk is real.

Do not allow it to deter you from making an assessment of it. Oh, by the way Growth is real also.

Second, once you have a broad idea of the goals you want to achieve, you can hone in on these goals by conducting research analyzing the performance of various financial instruments like stocks, mutual funds, bonds, debentures, etc., to provide you with a view of how the company is performing. It also helps in determining their future performance for price movements.

You will have an insight into the company's standing in the market, which helps you to decide whether investing in a particular company is viable or not. Your investment research helps in removing the information gap and letting you make more efficient and profitable decisions.

Consider collaborating using tools that can help you. Collaboration is easier when you have the right communication tools in place to do so. Use investment tools to share your goals and get feedback from your circle.

You will have to map out risks, your brainstorming risk scenarios in step one of your implementation strategy, and in step three, now you will map out all the potential risks you may face in your plan. Risks can include anything from loss of income and budget constraints.

Be flexible and proactive: Mapping out risks is more than just a preparation strategy. If you identify preventable risks during this stage of the implementation plan, you can take action to prevent those risks. This may mean adjusting your initial wealth creation goals.

Let me be very clear here, investing without knowledge opens the door to you falling for scams that increases your risk. So, it is vital to conduct thorough research before picking an investment avenue. For example, while investing in equity, check the company's growth, debt-to-equity ratio, etc., to analyze the company's future growth. This can help you avoid pitfalls. More on this later

Your risk appetite refers to your ability to tolerate risk in investment. Your risk tolerance or appetite can depend on your age and financial goals. Usually, younger investors tend to be more risk-tolerant than older ones.

If you are young, you can invest more in equity, which is a high-risk asset class. But if you are nearing retirement, try to invest more in fixed-income assets as they are considered relatively low-risk.

The fourth thing is you need to get a lot of "WIN's" established so scheduling your milestones is an important step in the planning process because these checkpoints help you track your progress during execution. Milestones serve as metrics— they are a way to measure how far you've come in your wealth creation and how far you have left to go.

Put It In Action

To visualize your goals, milestones and keep your entire household on track as you visually lay out your implementation schedule and show how long you think each task will take.

It's okay to add wiggle room if things don't always go as planned, even if you do everything in your power to a schedule. By adding wiggle room to your schedule, you can ensure your goals stay on track instead of keeping tight milestones and failing to meet them.

Over time I learned that if you clarify dependencies it will serve you well. Dependencies are nothing more than tasks that rely on the completion of other tasks. Clarifying your dependencies makes it easier to keep the project on track and hit your milestones.

The fifth step is to be sure that members of the household are assigned responsibilities and tasks. Every action plan must include a list of responsibilities with members assigned to each one. By assigning responsibilities, you can assess the performance of each member and monitor progress more closely.

Lastly, assigning responsibilities is different from assigning individual tasks. One member may be responsible for overseeing the goals review, while you may assign other members to handle the delivery and assets review. When you assign responsibilities and tasks, be sure to make your expectations clear.

When you assign roles, responsibilities, or tasks, it's best to communicate why you're choosing one member over another. Instead of letting members question why they have specific roles, you can use this step in the planning process as an opportunity to highlight member strengths.

Resource allocation is one of the best ways to reduce risk. If you can plan out what resources you need for your goals and ensure those resources will be available, you'll avoid the risk of running out of resources mid-way. If you notice that you don't have enough resources in this step of the implementation process, you can adjust your goals accordingly before it kicks off.

Looking at your asset allocation will involve dividing your investments among different assets, such as stocks, bonds, and cash. The asset allocation decision is a personal one. The allocation that works best for you changes at different times in your life, depending on how long you have to invest and your ability to tolerate risk.

Your time horizon is the number of months, years, or decades you need to invest to achieve your financial goal. If you have a longer time horizon you may feel comfortable taking on riskier or more volatile investments. Those with a shorter time horizon may prefer to take on less risk.

Following these steps as you create your implementation plan will increase the likelihood of hitting your wealth creation goals. You will determine things you can include in your implementation plan that will lead to successful implementation.

Once you are content with and feel good about the process, the implementation of the plan would be carried out. This step of the financial planning process can be considered as an action plan where you will pick ways to achieve your short, immediate or long term goals. Often taken as the toughest step for some people, but makes a huge difference in the long run!

The key thing to consider here is to carry it out as early as you can. The longer it's left unattended, the longer it will take you to grow your wealth – ultimately a great shortfall in your savings when you retire.

This is an on-going and dynamic process and it's unlikely that your financial condition will remain the same throughout your life. You need to assess your financial decisions periodically as changing personal, economic and social factors will require you to alter your decisions to fit into your new situation.

As you progress through the different phases of your life, your financial needs will be reflected and the financial process will serve as a tool to let you adjust to these changes.

Monitoring your plans will help you prioritize your decisions and make necessary adjustments that will bring your financial needs and goals in line with your current life situation.

Many aspects of implementation overlap with strategic planning. As a project manager, working on the project implementation plan while you are also working on the strategic plan can help minimize the total time spent on planning.

Another way to save time during the planning process is to house all of your plans in a work management platform. When your project team is ready to start the implementation process, everything is in one convenient place.

Now that you have the knowledge, knowing how to create your implementation plan is crucial, but you also need to know what to include in your plan. You will need to outline your wealth creation objectives in step one of the implementation process.

Set your goals and decide what metrics you will use to measure to monitor progress. By clearly identifying your wealth creation objectives, you can measure progress and performance as you move forward.

All of the steps undertaken to build each process to wealth creation will vary depending on the goals you are undertaking, and cannot therefore be described here in any real detail. The activities required to build each process must be clearly specified within the plan.

Your job as wealth creator is to direct the plan, but you need to do more than deliver the results. You also need to keep track of how well your household performs. The implementation phase keeps the plan on track with careful monitoring and control processes to ensure the final processes meet the acceptance criteria set by you.

When you have a problem and you very well may, you can't just make a change, because it may be too expensive or take too long to do. You will need to look at how it affects the triple

21

constraint (time, cost, scope) and how it impacts your wealth creation.

You will then have to figure out if it is worth making the change. If you evaluate the impact of the change and find that it won't have an impact on the plan triple constraint, then you can make the change without going through change control. Change control is a set of procedures you will learn about as you move forward it lets you make changes in an organized way.

Please remember that you are going to grow and adjust as you move forward to learning the process for you to become a true wealth creator. To my high income earners, to my advance investor please step back in your assessment of the direction and reimagine what is different is this process that can have.

These next few chapters will bring completely different applications to wealth creation that will change lives forever.

Chapter Three

Accumulation

Let's have the right understanding of why wealth accumulation is important. If you do not need wealth accumulation, then whatever you earn will go towards immediate spending. Common sense will alert you that this is not wise.

Wealth accumulation is the deliberate and disciplined process of accumulating assets to achieve certain meaningful goals. Without a clear goal, wealth accumulation is no different than wealth hoarding, producing more stresses and anxieties.

In order to accumulate wealth, it is necessary to position yourself with the right frame of mind and attitude that will allow you to work at achieving the financial freedom you desire. In my book series, including this book I have shared some tried and tested strategies to help you develop the right wealth creating mindset.

In developing the right mindset to create wealth it is important to know what your current mindset is. This knowledge will assist you in knowing what your mindset is and what you need to do to improve it.

It is very interesting how the little things that you don't even consider can influence and affect the way you think about wealth and assets.

Accumulation

Things like your childhood, how your parents talked about money around you, your environments, the kind of friends you have, your education and even advertisements that you are exposed to.

All these things play a role in your mindset. Unfortunately, we don't pause to think about why we behave the way we do.

Again, when you think of the rich what comes to mind? Do you think this is simply impossible to attain or you ask how did they make it?

While others think money is evil and therefore it is fine to have just enough for the day, others push themselves to make more to make a difference.

Asking yourself these questions gives you an idea where you currently are. Remember as a man thinks so is he, you cannot make more than you think, if you think small, small is what you birth.

If thinking small, births small then certainly thinking big would be better. A mindset that creates wealth must first believe wealth creation is possible and can be achieved no matter your current state.

Be ambitious in your dreams and aspirations. Think big and dream bigger because the world is full of possibilities and the opportunities do exist.

A mindset that creates wealth doesn't fear failure but only fears not trying at all. Discouragement and failure are two of the surest stepping stones to success, please understand you develop success from failures.

A lot of people fear these two. If you begin to see failure as a stepping stone, then you have the right mindset. If you begin to see failure, as giving you that push or motivation, then you are having a mindset shift that is bringing you closer to creating wealth.

You need to grow your money or better still put your money to work to create wealth. Setting some money aside is a great start, however your money needs to work for you. There is risk in putting your money to work.

It's comparatively safer to save your money in a money box at home or in a bank account, however you won't create wealth by simply saving and not taking any risk at all. A wealth creation mindset takes some risk, and undoubtedly what is comfortable.

A lot of times you may think you are either too young or too old to invest but that is never the case. You are never too young or too old to start creating wealth. A mindset that wins at wealth creation is one that simply gets it done.

Yes, the excuses sound good however if it is important to you, you will find a way and not an excuse. Do not wait for motivation, I'm told it's overrated, it might take too long or never come. Wake up every day determined to make money and just do it. The ideal mindset is positive. Surround yourself with positive minded people and eventually you will develop a similar mindset.

It is said if you walk with the wise you increase their number, in the same vein when you walk with those who have the right mindset, you develop one over time. You eventually become like the five-closest people in your circle so choose well.

Build a consistent mindset, not one that starts and stops halfway. Wealth is created over time with consistency so make sure one of the things you build is consistency.

Doing little things daily builds a habit which grows into a lifestyle and soon you will be amazed in a few years what you would have attained. Waiting to start off big may never happen, start by taking a small step daily to reach your goal.

A curious mind is a learning mind, to create wealth you need to keep learning and asking the right questions. Developing a curious mindset sets you off to creating wealth.

Be curious about those who have created wealth, read about how they came into wealth, ask questions on how you can also start creating wealth and with time it would happen.

It is important to have investment discussions with our children at a much younger age. As you develop a wealth creation mindset, carry them along.

This is how you develop the right mindset towards wealth creation. You set your goal, make the necessary enquiries and work towards achieving your goal.

People often think of wealth accumulation in different ways. What I want to do in this chapter is to provide you with the reasons you are to accumulate assets and things to create wealth.

If you have seen the lavish spending sprees and apartment tours on various TV shows, you've probably had a twinge of jealousy over how wealthy some people are - I know I have!

After all, most of us want to be rich rather than middle class. But wealth accumulation might be something you have not honestly thought about.

Ever thought how do you create wealth?
Is wealth accumulation only for the rich and famous?
Not at all!

Only a very few are born into it, many others spend a long time accumulating their wealth. And it is not as difficult as it might seem. In fact, 88% of millionaires made their money on their own without inheriting it.

I am going to provide you a process that will give you an equal opportunity as a wealth creator to establish generational wealth. But first you must learn some new ways of handling your money and what best to use your money on.

Let me start off by sharing with you that wealth accumulation is acquiring money, properties, or other assets that increase your net worth over time.

Accumulation

You can achieve it through investing and actively earning returns through them. Most people accumulate wealth to secure a financially stable future for years to come.

Listen, it is common for you to want a financially secure life, particularly after retirement. However, wealth accumulation differs for different individuals. It usually depends on your goals and aspirations.

The setting of long-term and short-term goals can help planning for the future. Having a long-term wealth accumulation plan will have a compounding effect.

Asset accumulation is building wealth over time by earning, saving, and investing money. It can be measured by the total dollar value of all assets, by the amount of income that is derived from the assets, or by the change in the total value of the assets over a period of time.

Asset accumulation typically refers to the acquisition of financial assets that represent value or yield income. The income may include interest payments, dividends, rents, royalties, fees, or capital gains.

These assets derive their value through a contractual claim rather than a tangible quality. Examples of non-physical financial instruments include stocks, bank deposits, and bonds.

Other forms of asset accumulation can also, less commonly, refer to the accumulation of the tangible means of production, such as factories or research and development, as well as physical assets, such as real estate.

For some of my readers the idea of wealth accumulation may not have an immediate connection to the processes for them and I want to challenge you to stay engaged. I will continue to repeat that wealth accumulation meaning may differ according to your individual goal.

It largely depends on the goals and aspirations of the individual. For some, it may be having enough wealth (income, money, and assets) that give you time, freedom, and returns. For some, it may mean having large amounts of money that can feed generations continually.

The main difference between being wealthy and rich in my opinion is that a rich person is rich until the money is exhausted. Wealthy people will have enough cash to satisfy their needs, and their investments continuously give returns to fulfill their goals.

However, there is no one particular wealth accumulation product that can make you wealthy.

You should have a clear idea of their short-term and long-term goals. Having a wealth accumulation plan is therefore important. The plan will conceptualize the goals, the ways, and means to achieve them, along with their timelines.

You must learn to employ various wealth accumulation strategies to form a perfect plan. These plans, like any other financial plan, involve investing which involves a factor of risk. Therefore care should be taken in formulating such plans.

Accumulation

Earning, investing, and building wealth typically occur during the 30s, 40s, and 50s, with a plan to retire comfortably by 60. You should want to retire much earlier than most people. You should adjust your wealth accumulation strategies accordingly.

You heard this before, (pun is intended) accumulating wealth involves cutting expenses, saving, investing, creating multiple income streams, etc. All these steps are taken with one focus—to live a financially stable, independent life.

Working all through one's life will not lead to financial freedom. The money invested has to create more money to achieve it. This will help in early retirement. The earlier you retire the less financial stress you have to go through.

It also creates assets that one can pass down to future generations. It also helps you achieve your goals and aspirations according to your timeline. This gives you a sense of satisfaction and helps you live a contented life.

Here is something to grab on to as you move forward, accumulation has two meanings for you and those saving for retirement. I am referring to the period when you are working and planning and ultimately building up the value of your investment through savings.

The accumulation phase is then followed by the distribution phase, in which once you retire you begin accessing and using your funds.

The accumulation phase essentially begins when you start saving money for retirement and ends when you begin taking distributions. For many people, this starts when you begin your working life and ends when you retire from the work world.

It is possible to start saving for retirement even before beginning the work phase of one's life, such as when someone is a student, but it is not common. Typically, joining the workforce coincides with the start of the accumulation phase.

Please understand that the sooner you begin the accumulation process, the better, with the long-term financial difference between beginning to save in your 20s vs. in the 30s substantial.

Postponing consumption by saving during an accumulation period will most often increase the amount of consumption one will be able to have later. The earlier the accumulation period is in your life, the more advantages you will have, such as compounding interest and protection.

In Chapter 5, I will talk about strategy and how to put various strategies in place for many products and purposes. So far, I have reminded you of what you and heard and known before. I believe that I have made this relatable to you and your household.

I know that when it comes to achieving your personal and business goals, money tends to be a great focus on measuring success. The wealth creation mindset is essentially your attitude towards cash, so developing a positive mindset about wealth creation is crucial for overall success and well-being.

To create a mindset around wealth creation and accumulation, you want to rid your mind of all limiting beliefs preventing you from taking action, then start looking at the world through an opportunistic lens to fully achieve abundance in your life.

I am pushing to change your mindset about wealth creation and make it your priority, but first you will want to understand what this mindset is. A wealth creation and accumulation mindset is an overriding attitude that you have about your finances.

Trust me when I say this, your mindset around money drives your financial decisions every day. This can have a huge impact on your ability to achieve your goals. It is vital for success to focus on having a positive mindset.

You already know that money can be a stressful topic for many. If you change your mindset about wealth creation you tend to make better choices about how to overcome challenges.

Wealth creation and mindset go hand and hand, so understanding it and focusing on ways to view it positively, is crucial for lifelong success.

I know I have not talked about this as much as I should have. There is something BIGGER happening here. When you fix your relationship with money, you will transform so many other areas of your life.

If you have never missed a credit card payment or bill, you might as well be a financial guru. However, for the vast majority of people it is important to forgive your financial mistakes.

The goal now is to shift your focus away from shame and make room for better practices and a more positive attitude towards wealth creation in the future. Forgiving yourself and financial mistakes, first acknowledge what happened, apologize to yourself, then focus on moving forward.

If you start to develop a negative mindset toward this process just remember, your financial mistakes are not you. You are independent of your financial mistakes in the past. Positive thinking means you are looking for solutions and expect to find them.

No, you don't ignore problems, but instead of complaining about them or letting them overpower you, you are actively looking for ways to overcome them. You take responsibility for your life on a consistent basis because you understand you are in control of how your life progresses.

For you to be successful I need you to be a positive thinker who finds the benefits — or the bright side — of challenges and expects things to work out well. Investing can and will at times seem intimidating. Think about it, you have been reading this series of books and you feel a rush of energy so let that be your sign that it works!

You must have an optimistic outlook. An optimistic attitude means you have hope. You believe things will work out well and ultimately you will have success. Negativity will come, not always from outside but from within. Let me show you some ways you can replace pessimistic thoughts with positive thoughts:

Instead of saying, "I don't want to do that, I've never done it before," say, "I'll try it because I may learn something new."

Instead of thinking, "I'm never going to get better at this," say, "I'll try again until I figure it out."

We tend to be hard on ourselves, but we need to be our biggest cheerleaders.

So when you feel you've made a mistake or even failed at this process, think instead, "What can I learn from this so that I'll be more successful?" Don't think about what if you fail, think about what if you succeed.

Now it's time for a new Blueprint!

Chapter Four

Compounding Effect

Now I want to talk about a process of wealth creation that some may see as a strategy. This process can be extremely powerful for your wealth creation or in most cases it is also a devastating tool that can destroy your wealth. It just depends on which side of the financial equation you use it.

I want to get the negative side of this process on the table first. As I talk about the negative side of the process please understand that it is not to condemn the banking system or even credit cards or any other financial product.

Many of my colleagues make a living by teaching financial fear. I am sure that you have heard that you should not put your money in the banking system because they take your money and use your money to make money for themselves.

It is a business fact that banks use deposits and make investment in lending that earns them lots of money and they only give you a very small fraction for the use of your money. I have to be clear, if you never have more than $250.00 in the bank at any giving time, do not even worry about it.

I have to say this, it is funny how the majority of the people I hear repeating this business fact are people who do not have any real money (meaning average daily balance of $1500.00 or more) in the bank. It is sad when my colleagues tell readers that you can never create wealth in the banking system.

The banking system was never designed to create wealth. However, it is a vital source of your financial growth and your ability to function in our society. It is the foundation of all wealth creation in the sense of having a stable place to harvest your money. Your growth we will talk about later in the book.

The other part to the negative side of this process is that it makes debt (e.g. credit cards) grow quicker and more significantly over time. What am I talking about? It is interest! It's compound interest to be exact.

You might have learned about compound interest as a kid when you opened a savings account and the bank added it to your balance every month. As pleasing as it is to earn money for doing nothing more than keeping it in an account, you probably have learned that compound interest is a double-edged sword.

Banks are in business to borrow your money at a low rate and lend it at a higher one. Deposits are one way banks borrow. They pay you for the right to use your deposits to make loans.

They use compound interest on both ends of the equation, paying depositors and charging borrowers, and make money on the spread – the difference between the interest they pay depositors and the interest they charge borrowers is bank revenue.

Most of us are on both sides of the equation. We earn interest on checking and savings accounts, and we pay interest on mortgages, car loans and credit card balances.

The key is what financiers call the "time value of money." The longer your money is in the bank, the more it grows. As interest is added to the balance, you have a larger balance and earn more interest. But if you're borrowing money, say with a credit card, the reverse is true.

Please remember this term going forward, it is your power drill to wealth creation "time value on money." (TVM)

I have said this in many of my other books, the math for compound interest is simple: Principal x interest = new balance.

For example, a $10,000 investment that returns 8% every year, is worth $10,800 ($10,000 principal x .08 interest = $10,800) after the first year. It grows to $11,664 ($10,800 principal x .08 interest = $11,664) at the end of the second year.

In 25 years, that initial investment of $10,000 would grow to $68,484, thanks to compound interest. That is so awesome, excellent growth. Unfortunately, the same math applies to credit card debt, only in a very negative way.

The average credit card interest rate in the spring of 2018 was 17% APR. If you owe $5,000 in credit card debt and make only the 4% minimum payment due (-$200), you would have

$71 of interest added to your balance so you would now owe the card company $4,871.

If you didn't use that card at all, and continued to pay the 4% minimum every month, it would take 10 years and 10 months) to pay off the debt. You would pay a total of $7,627 – including $2,627 of interest – to pay off what started out as a $5,000 debt. That is the negative power of compound interest!

Interest rates are often defined as the price paid to borrow money. For example, an annualized 2% interest rate on a $100 loan means that the borrower must repay the initial loan amount plus an additional $2 after one full year.

So what does it mean when you have a negative interest rate—meaning borrowers are credited interest, instead of being charged it? That, say, a -2% interest rate means the bank pays the borrower $2 after a year of using the $100 loan?

Remember with negative interest rates, cash deposited at a bank yields a storage charge, rather than the opportunity to earn interest income; the idea is to incentivize loaning and spending, rather than saving and hoarding.

Now that all of that is out of the way, you want to know what's in it for you right. Well, on the positive side, compound interest makes a return on investments (e.g. savings, retirement accounts) grow quicker over time.

When you deposit money into a savings account, the bank pays you interest. Over time, the interest you earn increases your principal or the amount you're earning interest on. And as your principal grows, so does the amount of interest you earn on it, creating a flywheel that can grow your money further.

How frequently your interest compounds is a key factor here; daily compounding will increase your balance the quickest, but some banks compound on a monthly, quarterly or annual basis.

Investing your money can appear extremely complicated and time-consuming but, once you've mastered your current financial situation, it can help you take your finances to the next level.

After working my first corporate job, I found myself wanting to invest some of my earnings but was unsure where to start. I had never made any investments before. I thought investing was only something done by professional financial advisors or big corporations. I was really at a loss about where to begin.

At the same time, I didn't want to leave my earnings in a simple savings account because I knew that it could reduce my purchasing power over time.

Most savings accounts have interest rates lower than the rate of inflation, so I knew I was at risk to lose some money. I realized that I had to do something.

So how does a country boy who doesn't know much, go about investing any extra cash I may have? Well, I can tell you what I thought were the most logical steps to take: I looked up articles and guides about how to start investing in stocks and bonds.

Through these readings, I realized that, given my limited knowledge base, I had little interest in actively managing and selecting individual stocks and bonds. So, I turned to learn about passive investments (which select the stocks for you) such as mutual funds.

Once I read up on mutual funds, I learned what a brokerage account was and how to open the account.

After going through that research process, I decided to open a brokerage account and invest in mutual funds. I was provided with suggestions about different mutual funds and selected one that was well diversified (it owned stocks in companies across different industries) and had a decent expected return.

Again, since I was choosing to passively manage my money, I wasn't checking the status of my investments every day but rather every couple weeks or whenever big news stories appeared. When I reflect back on my initial investing experience, I realized one big takeaway: the power of compound interest.

When you invest, your account earns compound interest. This means, not only will you earn money on the principal amount in your account, but you will also earn interest on the accrued interest you've already earned.

The idea of compound interest (as compared to simple interest) is fundamental to investing because it can ultimately lead to a greater return in your account.

Here is an example that is very basic, something that you probably have seen before. But I want you to start allowing this example to make sense to you.

You may invest $1000 into a mutual fund and receive an 8% return, during the course of a year, leaving you with an account balance of $1080.

Now, with compound interest, if you decide to invest the $1080 into the mutual fund with an 8% return, you will have an account balance of $1,166.40 after the second year.

This is different than if you just earned the simple 8% interest on the principal amount of $1000 which would leave you with an account balance of $1160 after two years.

Now, just think about if you invested over your whole professional career (assume 35 years) and continued to earn compound interest, you would be returning A LOT of money to your wallet!

All of this is to say, investing can be incredibly beneficial to securing your financial success and wealth creation.

My advice to you: If you're nervous about investing for the first time and scared about losing your money in the market, that's extremely valid and okay.

With that in mind, you may want to begin investing as early as your financial situation allows for so that you can reap the benefits of compound interest.

Ultimately, how you invest is up to you and your preferences. Above all, I'd encourage you to be mindful of your current financial situation and your risk tolerance for investing.

Compound interest is the interest on a deposit calculated based on both the initial principal and the accumulated interest from previous periods.

Or, more simply put, compound interest is interest you earn on interest. You can compound interest on different frequency schedules such as daily, monthly or annually.

Your money makes money on the money that your money already made, it becomes a vicious cycle. Yet a very doggone good cycle my friend.

So many people are seeking ways to make money other than allowing money to make money for them. They are too busy trying to get use of other people's money.

The higher the number of compounding periods, the greater the compounded interest that is earned. Think about it like a snowball. The sooner you start saving, and the more money you add to your snowball, the larger it will grow.

Now, think about if you pushed the snowball down a snow-covered hill. Now the snow you already packed will stay, and you'll accumulate more snow.

Eventually, when your snowball reaches the bottom of the hill, it will contain the snow you started with, the snow it picked up along the way, and even more snow on top of that.

In other words, the interest-on-interest effect can generate continually increasing returns based on your initial investment amount.

So, the more frequently you save, and the larger the amount you save, will return larger amounts of interest. This is also called "the miracle of compound interest."

Believe me when I tell you compound interest causes your wealth to grow faster. It makes a sum of money grow at a faster

43

rate than simple interest because you will earn returns on the money you invest, as well as on returns at the end of every compounding period.

Some would say that this means you don't have to put away as much money to reach your goals. The larger the investment the larger the return, remember time also plays a role.

There are concepts that explain how you can save $1000 a year for 6 years and never put any more money into the investment. I can start when you stop and can never match your investment if I did $1000 every year afterwards. (TVM)

The magic of compounding can be an important factor when building your wealth. The earlier you open an interest-bearing account and start stocking away money, the more money you will earn in compound interest.

It's also key to helping mitigate wealth-eroding factors like the rising cost of living, inflation, and reduction of purchasing power.

Some financial experts suggest that you may need one million dollars to retire comfortably. Of course, this depends on your living expenses, what you consider a comfortable life, and how long retirement will last for you.

For people who come from money, this might not seem like a lofty goal. For those who work normal jobs (and even living paycheck-to-paycheck), the idea of becoming a millionaire may feel like a far-off dream.

If you're in that second category, this is why I am talking about compound interest. Is it possible that it can turn you into a millionaire if you play your cards right?

It's important for me to continue to point out and make clear to you about this process of compound interest. When you understand the importance of having your money work to make money for you it should become automatic for you.

In basic terms, compound interest is "interest on interest." It's the total of all of the interest value combined with the principal (the original sum of money that goes into a loan or investment) minus the present value of the principal.

Simple interest is only based on the initial amount of money that someone invests. Compound interest adds together all of the money that accumulates because of the building interest. In other words, you reinvest the small amount of money that you get as interest, and it builds up over time.

The younger you are (and thus the more time you have to accrue interest), the more compound interest can benefit you in the long run as long as you're willing and able to leave your money untouched. The sooner you start investing for retirement, the better off you'll be.

The Compound Effect

While this seems like slow growth, that slow growth adds up over time. Of course, you should be planning to add more money to that investment as well.

Compounding isn't a replacement for continuing to add money to your investment account. It's a way to make that money grow more quickly without any extra effort or risk.

I hate saying it this way because I believe that you will be a creator of wealth going forward. However, whether or not you become a millionaire will depend on how much money you're able to invest.

At the end of the day, compound interest will get you closer to becoming a millionaire than simple interest, and if you're able to put aside even $5 per day into an account with an 8% return, you'll have over one million dollars in 50 years. If you're able to invest more than that, the process will be much quicker.

There is awesome power in compounding interest and it can turn meager investments into wealth creation over time, but only if you start investing as soon as possible and then stay invested. Staying invested is key to maximizing the effects of compound interest.

PLEASE HEAR THIS, if you are constantly moving or withdrawing your money whenever the market declines, you lose out on a lot of potential compounded interest. There is no paying yourself back going on here.

Staying invested can be hard through market drawdowns. If you have a portfolio worth $100,000 and the market drops 20%, it looks as if you lost $20,000. But keep in mind that there are no true losses until you make the decision to sell.

If you focus on buying strong businesses that can persist through periods of bad economic performance, the prices will rebound over time. I will be talking about products later in the book.

Too often, investors are scared off by the drawdown and sell, only to then miss the bounce and buy back the stocks once the price has recovered.

Speaking of stock, I will talk about products later in the book. But I want to give you a sense of what and how you can and should work with them.

There are various types of accounts that offer compound interest. You have several options for taking advantage of compounding interest to build wealth. Each of these investing strategies generates compound interest:

Savings accounts: Banks lend out the cash that you put into a savings account and pay you interest in exchange for not withdrawing the funds.

Savings accounts that compound daily, as opposed to weekly or monthly, are the best because frequently compounding interest increases your account balance faster. You can open a savings account with any local or online bank.

Money market accounts: These are mostly the same as savings accounts, except money market accounts allow you to write checks and make ATM withdrawals.

Money market accounts often pay slightly higher interest rates than savings accounts. The downsides of money market accounts are that most limit the number of transactions you can complete each month and some charge a fee if your balance falls below a certain amount.

Zero-coupon bonds: These bonds generate the equivalent of compound interest to compensate for the risk associated with holding zero-coupon bonds.

A zero-coupon bond holder purchases a bond at a steep discount, receives no interest payments (coupons) in exchange for holding the bond, and is paid the bond's face value when the bond is due. There is a risk that the company may not be able to repay the bond's full face value at the end of the term.

Dividend stocks: Stocks that pay dividends generate compound interest if you reinvest the dividends. You can instruct your brokerage to automatically reinvest all dividend payments you receive and buy more shares.

While savings accounts and money market accounts are both extremely safe options, you are unlikely to find an account that pays even 1% interest.

To significantly profit from compounding interest, it's important to diversify your money with different types of accounts and investments.

Compound interest is great when it works in your favor in investments, but it can also be your biggest enemy when it works against you in loans and other debts.

The key is to figure out how you can let it work in your favor. If you stay on top of your loan payments and always keep an eye on your investments, then compound interest can be your best friend when it comes to wealth.

Having control of your personal finances makes it easier to navigate the road as you look towards the future.

Next I want to really talk about strategy and how it is where you will focus your efforts to achieve your goals, and how you will succeed—or, "where to play and how to win." It defines a specific course of action that will take you from where you are now to where you want to be.

I see a lot of strategies that resemble missions, visions, or BHGs (big hairy goals). If a strategy statement is too all-encompassing, you get caught on the hamster wheel of trying to do everything all at once, which often results in a lot of busy work. In fact, one of strategy's primary roles is to set constraints on the work you'll do.

The Compound Effect

Just another glance at what compound can do for you. Let's say you want to start savings out of the money earned by you. You decide to deposit the initial amount of $ 10,000 into the high-interest account. The rate of interest, in this case, will be 15 % per annum compounded yearly. Currently, you are 25 years old, and your plans are to see what it look like over 20 years. One single deposit! Imagine every 2 years another 10K deposit!

Year	Interest	Account Value
0		$10,000.00
1	$1,500.00	$11,500.00
2	$1,725.00	$13,225.00
3	$1,983.75	$15,208.75
4	$2,281.31	$17,490.06
5	$2,623.51	$20,113.57
6	$3,017.04	$23,130.61
7	$3,469.59	$26,600.20
8	$3,990.03	$30,590.23
9	$4,588.53	$35,178.76
10	$5,276.81	$40,455.58
11	$6,068.34	$46,523.91
12	$6,978.59	$53,502.50
13	$8,025.38	$61,527.88
14	$9,229.18	$70,757.06
15	$10,613.56	$81,370.62
16	$12,205.59	$93,576.21
17	$14,036.43	$107,612.64
18	$16,141.90	$123,754.54
19	$18,563.18	$142,317.72
20	$21,347.66	$163,665.37

Chapter Five

Strategy

This chapter will probably get scrutinized more than any of the other books, even by people who do not choose to follow any of the principles that I teach. What I want for you the reader to do is stop reading right now after these instructions.

If you have been into the series from the mindset forward, this is where I need you to trust me. I have intentionally written this series to get you to this point. Now, I need you to stop reading and begin to reimagine the reason you picked up the first book.

I need you to trust your gut feelings and focus on wealth creation like never before. The information may not be all that new to you, but it is new to you in your new mindset about wealth creation. It is time to see it all differently.

The reason you need to stop reading is to clear your mind completely from the old way of thinking. Put aside any preconceived thoughts and ideas and be intentionally intentional about your wealth creation journey. NOW STOP READING HERE!

Strategy

Now that you have cleared your mind let's begin with some of the first steps in creating a strategy that fits your profit objectives, skills and values.

Your understanding that an investment strategy is a set of principles that guides investment decisions. There are several different investing plans you can follow depending on your risk tolerance, investing style, long-term financial goals, and access to capital.

I am going to list five or more investing strategies that are flexible. If you choose one and it doesn't suit your risk tolerance or schedule, you can certainly make changes. However, changing investment strategies can come at a cost.

Each time you buy or sell securities—especially in the short-term in non-sheltered accounts— it may create taxable events. You may also realize your portfolio is riskier than you'd prefer after your investments have dropped in value.

Here, I want to start off looking at four common investing strategies that suit most investors. By taking the time to understand the characteristics of each, you will be in a better position to choose one that's right for you over the long term without the need to incur the expense of changing course.

Nuggets

Before you figure out your strategy, take some notes about your financial situation and goals. If you have been reading the series, you should have done this work already. Know that value investing requires you to remain in it for the long term and to apply effort and research to your stock selection.

If you follow growth strategies you should be watchful of executive teams and news about the economy. If you are a momentum investor you will be buying stocks experiencing an uptrend and may choose to short sell those securities.

Dollar-cost averaging is the practice of making regular investments in the market over time. Before you begin to research your investment strategy, it's important to gather some basic information about your financial situation.

Ask yourself these key questions if you have not already:
What is your current financial situation?
What is your cost of living including monthly expenses and debts?
How much can you afford to invest—both initially and on an ongoing basis?

Even though you don't need a lot of money to get started, you shouldn't start investing until you can afford to do so. If you cannot save money and leave it there STOP and go get on a budget.

If you have debts or other obligations, consider the impact investing will have on your short-term cash flow before you start putting money into your portfolio.

I know you want to get started investing, remember if you cannot afford to lose the money you invest don't do it. If you are

Strategy

looking only short term and may need this money down the road don't do it. This is the part that gives you the impression that investing is risky. It is to those who probably should not be doing it in the first place.

Listen, make sure you can afford to invest before you actually start putting money away. Prioritize your current obligations before setting money aside for the future.

Again, this should have already been done, set out your goals. Everyone has different needs, so you should determine what yours are. Are you saving for retirement? Are you looking to make big purchases like a home or car in the future?

Are you saving for your or your children's education? This will help you narrow down a strategy as different investment approaches have different levels of liquidity, opportunity, and risk. You may need to use more than one strategy.

You have to figure out what your risk tolerance is. Your risk tolerance is determined by two things. What? Did I say two things? First, this is normally determined by several key factors including your age, income, and how long you have until you retire.

If you are younger you have time on your side to recuperate losses, so it's often recommended that younger investors hold more risk than those who are older.

Risk tolerance is also a highly-psychological aspect to investing largely determined by your emotions. How would you

54

feel if your investments dropped 30% overnight? How would you react if your portfolio is worth $1,000 less today than yesterday?

Sometimes, the best strategy for making money makes people emotionally uncomfortable. If you're constantly worrying about the state of possibly losing money, chances are your portfolio has too much risk. Look, I have a completely different approach to things that impacts my emotions.

In the early eighties I earned a black belt in martial arts, the style I took was called Savate. There many times I would put myself at what would be considered high risk only because I was young and knew that I could kick some apple sauce sauce out of people.

This was a calculated risk based on the fact that I had in my knowledge bank. However, today I would not take such a risk, because of my age and the fact that guns are the primary source of solving disputes. Like with investing, if you get the knowledge you can minimize the risk.

Risk isn't necessarily bad in investing. Higher risk investments are often rewarded with higher returns. While lower risk investments are more likely to preserve their value, they also don't have the upside potential.

You are going to have to learn the basics of investing. Learn how to read stock charts, and begin by picking some of your favorite companies and analyzing their financial statements.

Strategy

Keep in touch with recent news about industries you're interested in investing in. It's a good idea to have a basic understanding of what you're getting into so you're not investing blindly.

As you begin to build out strategy you are going to notice a big difference in yourself in how you think and feel about the process. Money is beginning to take on a new meaning for you, you already are experiencing new behaviors or should I say new habits with money.

It is quite alright to enjoy positive emotions like gratitude, compassion, and pride. It will encourage you to be more persistent in reaching your goals—and help you stay away from dissenting behavior—they all have another benefit: nourishing our social relationships, which leads to more success and happiness.

In fact, this is the primary reason socially oriented emotions that build self-control exist in the first place: You will foster social connection, which often requires cooperation and self-sacrifice.

Cultivating these states in YOU will increase your motivation to act in ways that benefit others, including your own future. So, if you really want to persevere, stop trying to push through with willpower. Instead, start practicing gratitude, compassion, and pride. You—and those around you—will be glad you did.

You are really in a different place now.

Always remember that investment strategies are a set of claims that help you achieve your investment and financial goals. The strategies are formulated based on your financial goals, risk tolerance, and target. They are also formulated keeping your short-term goals and long-term goals in mind.

These strategies can be curated by you as well as the portfolio managers. Sometimes the strategies need to be changed as and when required as per the circumstances, as a static strategy would not be feasible for every circumstance.

Okay I think you get the point about where your head and action should be. I am about to talk about nine different strategies that have impacted my life making me the first link of generational wealth to be passed down. With your patience and focus I believe that you will go beyond any current dreams that you have.

Here are the nine different types of Investment Strategies that I believe will change the speed of wealth creation:

Passive and Active Strategies
Value Investing
Growth Investing (Short-Term and Long-Term Investments)
Income Investing
Socially Responsible Investing
Dividend Growth Investing
Contrarian Investing
Small-Cap Investing
Indexing

Passive and Active Strategies

Passive investing broadly refers to a buy-and-hold portfolio strategy for long-term investment with minimal trading in the market. Index investing is perhaps the most common form of passive investing, whereby you seek to replicate and hold a broad market index or indices.

Passive investment is cheaper, less complex, and often produces superior after-tax results over medium to long time horizons than actively managed portfolios.

Passive investing methods seek to avoid the fees and limited performance that may occur with frequent trading. Passive investing's goal is to build wealth gradually. Also known as a buy-and-hold strategy, passive investing means buying a security to own it long-term.

Unlike active traders, passive investors do not seek to profit from short-term price fluctuations or market timing. The underlying assumption of passive investment strategy is that the market posts positive returns over time.

The introduction of index funds in the 1970s made achieving returns in line with the market much easier. In the 1990s, exchange-traded funds, or ETFs, that track major indices, such as the SPDR S&P 500 ETF (SPY), simplified the process even further by allowing investors to trade index funds as though they were stocks. Yes

You can maintain a well-diversified portfolio is important to successful investing, and passive investing via indexing is an excellent way to achieve diversification. Index funds spread risk broadly in holding all, or a representative sample of the securities in their target benchmarks.

Index funds track a target benchmark or index rather than seeking winners, so they avoid constantly buying and selling securities. As a result, they have lower fees and operating expenses than actively managed funds.

An index fund offers simplicity as an easy way to invest in a chosen market because it seeks to track an index. There is no need to select and monitor individual managers, or choose among investment themes.

However, passive investing is subject to total market risk. Index funds track the entire market, so when the overall stock market or bond prices fall, so do index funds. Another risk is the lack of flexibility.

Index fund managers usually are prohibited from using defensive measures such as reducing a position in shares, even if the manager thinks share prices will decline.

Passively managed index funds face performance constraints as they are designed to provide returns that closely track their benchmark index, rather than seek outperformance. They rarely beat the return on the index, and usually return slightly less due to fund operating costs.

Strategy

Active investing refers to an investment strategy that involves ongoing buying and selling activity by you and your manager. Active investors purchase investments and continuously monitor their activity to exploit profitable conditions.

Please understand that active investing is highly involved. Unlike passive investors, who invest in a stock when they believe in its potential for long-term appreciation, active investors typically look at the price movements of their stocks many times a day.

Usually, active investors are seeking short-term profits. Smart beta exchange-traded funds are a cost-effective way for you to take advantage of active investing by considering alternative factors as opposed to simply tracking a benchmark index, such as selecting a portfolio based on company earnings or some other fundamental approach.

Active investing allows money managers to adjust investors' portfolios to align with prevailing market conditions. For example, during the height of a recent financial crisis, investment managers could have adjusted portfolio exposure to the financial sector to reduce their clients' risk in the market.

You can use active investing to take advantage of short-term trading opportunities. Traders can use swing trading strategies to trade market ranges or take advantage of the momentum.

Positions in swing trades are typically held between two and six days but may last as long as two weeks. Stock prices oscillate for the majority of the time which creates many short-term trading opportunities.

Active investing allows money managers to meet the specific needs of their clients, such as providing diversification, retirement income or a targeted investment return. For instance, a hedge fund manager might use an active long/short strategy in an attempt to deliver an absolute return that does not compare to a benchmark or other measure.

Limitations of active investing can be costly due to the potential for numerous transactions. If you are continually buying and selling stocks, commissions may significantly impact the overall investment return.

If you invest with an active investment manager, such as a hedge fund, typically have to pay a management fee, regardless of how successfully the fund performs.

Active management fees can range from 0.10% to over 2% of assets under management (AUM). Active money managers may also charge a performance fee between 10% and 20% of the profit they generate.

These active funds often set minimum investment thresholds for prospective investors. For example, a hedge fund might require new investors to make a starting investment of $250,000.

Value Investing

In the 1920s, Benjamin Graham developed a new method of investing in stocks called value investing, which was then made famous by Warren Buffet. To apply this strategy, one has to have a deep understanding of the stock market, as intensive research needs to be done.

In this strategy, you must seek out stocks that are being traded that do not comply with their intrinsic value. There can be two cases under this- overvaluation and undervaluation.

Overvaluation refers to the situation when a stock's trading price is higher than its intrinsic price, and undervaluation refers to the situation when the stock's trading price is lower than its intrinsic price.

You purchase stocks when they are undervalued and sell them when the stocks reach their intrinsic value or higher. You have to be patient and wait till the price of the share rises, which may be after a year or a few years.

Value investing strategy involves investing in the company by looking at its intrinsic value because such companies are undervalued by the stock market.

The idea behind investing in such companies is that when the market goes for correction, it will correct the value for such undervalued companies, and the price will then shoot up, leaving you with high returns when you sell. This strategy is used by the very famous Warren Buffet.

The advantages of value investing is the risk minimization- Usually, equity stocks are associated with high risks but, in the value investing method, you earmark the undervalued stocks and buy the potent shares on sale, thereby reducing the associated risks. You use margin of safety to reduce the risk. When these shares are sold at their intrinsic value or more, you receive substantial capital gains.

Growth Investment

This strategy focuses on capital increment. You employing this strategy usually purchase stocks of companies that exhibit signs of above-average earnings increments relative to the market or their industry sector. Usually, these companies are young or small and emerging with high prospective returns, posing a higher risk.

Since you aim for capital appreciation, most growth-stock companies reinvest their earnings instead of paying their shareholders dividends.

If the company is assumed to have a higher potential of prospering, the stocks are traded at a high price/earnings (P/E) ratio, with the hopes of higher stock prices in the future as they are expected to perform better in the future.

Usually, these companies hold patents or have access to technologies that put them ahead in the industry and ensure long term growth.

Strategy

You chose the holding period based on the value you want to create in your portfolio. If you believe that a company will grow in the coming years and the intrinsic value of a stock will go up, you should invest in such companies to build your corpus value.

This is also known as growth investing. On the other hand, if you believe that a company will deliver good value in a year or two, you should go for short term holding.

The holding period also depends upon the preference you have. For example, how soon you want money to buy a house, school education for kids, retirement plans, etc.

As I said earlier, you can have more than one strategy.

Income Investing

This strategy is focused on generating a regular stream of income. I know you like to hear this part, regular streams of income. Usually, these types of portfolios include bonds, stocks, Real Estate Investment Trusts (REITs), exchange-traded funds (ETFs), and other such investment instruments that produce the highest passive annual income. The incomes are usually dividends, bond yields, and interest returns and involve minimal risks.

This type of strategy focuses on generating cash income from stocks rather than investing in stocks that only increase the value of your portfolio. There are two types of cash income which you can earn – (1) Dividend and (2) Fixed interest income from bonds. If you are looking for steady income from investments opt for such a strategy.

A supplement of fixed income-It is an excellent way of earning extra income through one's own assets to supplement their permanent income.

Potential for growth of capital stock-In the long term, income investing strategies generate a potential for capital stock growth, eventually adding to one's stock of wealth.

Socially Responsible Investing

In this investment strategy, investments are made, considering the social impact and the impact on the environment. Usually, investments are made in companies engaged in socially conscious activities such as social justice, alternative energies, clean technologies, environmental sustainability, etc. Investments are not made in companies that have a negative impact on society- like cigarette manufacturing companies, companies offering gambling services, etc.

The two primary goals of a socially responsible investing strategy are financial gain and social impact. One might not be able to achieve both together, as a socially conscious investment might not provide good returns, and an investment in a company with good returns might not have socially conscious principles.

Hence, you need to read through the fund's brochure and determine the portfolio manager's philosophies. I personally love Cannabis

Dividend Growth Investing

In this type of investment strategy, the investor looks out for companies that consistently paid a dividend every year. Companies that have a track record of paying dividends consistently are stable and less volatile compared to other companies and aim to increase their dividend payout every year. The investors reinvest such dividends and benefit from compounding over the long term.

You should be looking to diversify your portfolio, hedge against market downturns and inflation, or potentially generate passive income may turn to dividend growth investments.

The companies offering these types of stocks are often recognized as being stable, low volatility, and even having a positive future outlook. As with any investment, however, dividend growth stocks still come with risks and considerations to keep in mind.

These dividends may be paid in cash via a dividend check or as a credit with a brokerage of choice, or as additional shares of stock. If paid in cash, you should reinvest it to purchase more shares or use that money elsewhere.

Dividend growth investing is a popular strategy with many current investors. It entails buying shares in companies with a record of paying regular and increasing dividends.

An added component is using the payouts to reinvest in the company's shares—or shares of other companies with similar dividend track records. <u>The goal is compound investment portfolio growth.</u> Although dividend growth investments are generally recognized as low volatility, no investment (or dividend payment) is guaranteed.

Contrarian Investing

This type of strategy allows you to buy stocks of companies at the time of the down market. This strategy focuses on buying at low and selling at high. The downtime in the stock market is usually at the time of recession, wartime, calamity, etc.

However, you shouldn't just buy stocks of any company during downtime. You should look out for companies that have the capacity to build up value and have a branding that prevents access to their competition.

Contrarian investing is an investment strategy that involves bucking against existing market trends to generate profits. The idea is that markets are subject to herding behavior augmented by fear and greed, making markets periodically over- and underpriced.

The contrarian sees buying opportunities in stocks that are currently selling for below their intrinsic value. Being a contrarian can be rewarding, but it is often a risky strategy that may take a long period of time to pay off.

Another drawback associated with being a contrarian investor is the need to spend a good deal of time researching stocks to find undervalued opportunities.

Small-Cap Investing

Small-cap investing strategy refers to investments made in stocks of small companies that have smaller market capitalization, usually between $300 million and $2 billion.

These investments are risky. The appeal of these stocks lies in the fact that, unlike large-cap stocks that have high prices due to being noticed by everyone, investors usually stay away from these stocks due to their riskiness and because there are restrictions on investment by institutional investors.

Hence, you have to be well-versed with the stock market investment as these stocks are quite volatile and difficult to trade.

Growth Potential-Most large-cap companies were once small businesses. The new emerging companies bring new products and services to the market and sometimes even create entirely new markets. Since these companies have lower total value, they can grow in manners, unlike large-cap companies.

Restrictions on investment by mutual funds-Mutual Funds usually invest large amounts that small-cap companies cannot support. For the investment to impact the fund's performance, the portfolio manager has to buy at least twenty per cent of the shares.

The SEC or Securities and Exchange Commission has introduced restrictions such that mutual funds cannot establish such prominent positions, giving individual investors an advantage to pick on promising companies before the institutional investors can.

Small-cap Value Index Funds- Small-cap value stocks are mostly unnoticed by the stock market investors and are undervalued, giving them larger returns. The best small-cap value index funds help get higher returns. Hence, choosing a strategy for investment requires a thorough understanding of your goals and which suits your needs best.

Indexing

This type of investment strategy allows you to invest a small portion of stocks in a market index. These can be S&P 500, mutual funds, exchange-traded funds.

Index investing is a hands-off investment approach that can be used by you with long-term goals. Index investing encompasses investing in a portfolio of assets that mimic a particular index or financial market. It allows you to own portions of stocks in many companies, all through one fund. Index funds have

They are also less expensive than their actively managed counterparts. It also offers scope for wider diversification. Index investing does not require the active management of stocks and is, therefore, passive investing is more viable through this form of investing as you do not have to spend your time and efforts on a regular basis to track the performances.

Investing Tips

Here are a few investing tips which should be kept in mind before investing.

Set Goals: Set goals on how much money is required by you in the coming period. This will allow you to set your mind straight whether you need to invest in long-term or short-term investments and how much return is to be expected.

Research and Trend Analysis: Get your research right in terms of understanding how the stock market works and how different types of instruments work (equity, bonds, options, derivatives, mutual funds, etc.). Also, research and follow the price and return trends of stocks you chose to invest.

Portfolio Optimization: Select the best portfolio out of the set of portfolios which meet your objective. The portfolio which gives maximum return at the lowest possible risk is an ideal portfolio.

Best Advisor/Consultancy: Find yourself a good consulting firm or brokerage firm. They will guide and give consultation regarding where and how to invest so that you meet your investment objectives.

Risk Tolerance: Know how much risk you are willing to tolerate to get the desired return. This also depends on your short term and long term goals. If you are looking for a higher return in a short period of time, the risk would be higher and vice versa.

Diversify Risk: Create a portfolio that is a mix of debt, equity, and derivatives so that the risk is diversified. Also, ensure that the two securities are not perfectly correlated to each other.

Some of the advantages to you using investment strategies allow for diversification of risk in the portfolio by investing in different types of investments and industry based on timing and expected returns.

A portfolio can be made of a single strategy or a combination of strategies to accommodate the preferences and needs that you may have. Investing strategically allows you to gain maximum out of your investments. Investment strategies help reduce transaction costs and pay less tax.

Listen, do not take it personally if you find it difficult to outperform the market. To earn an average return from investments, it may take you years, whereas professional investors would earn the same return in weeks or months. But let this be your goal as well for weeks or months.

Even though a lot of research, analysis, and historical data are considered before investing, most of the decisions are taken on a predictive basis. Sometimes, the results and returns may not be as it was anticipated, and it may delay you from achieving your goals.

It is very important to have an investment strategy. It will help you rule out poor portfolios and will increase the chances of success.

Strategy

Ask yourself a few basic questions like how much I want to invest?

How much return do I need?

How much is my risk tolerance?

What will be my investment horizon?

Why did I need to invest? Etc.

The clearer you are with your objectives, the better decision you will make regarding your investment. Always lookout for good opportunities and never invest at one go. Building a portfolio is like building a house brick by brick, money by money.

Chapter Six

Your Portfolio

I woke up this morning wondering what I should write, no, what I should start with. So I remember this story that captured my attention about a lady who got attached to a genre and formed a habit. When you hear her tell her story she has not met a Snoopy she has not liked.

Her interest in the happy-go-lucky beagle—a well-known member of the Peanuts comic strip gang—began back when she was in college. Her collection is now in the high hundreds. Snoopy paraphernalia can be found in her office, home, and car. His image also graces four watches, socks, tons of T-shirts, and a lot more.

She was quoted "I remember looking at something with Snoopy and it just cheered me up," she said. "I am an avid dog lover and Snoopy was a cartoon dog. I am also a Type A personality. And he is laid back, cool, and kind of goes with the flow. He is everything I am not, but I want to be."

Then I started thinking about myself and how I am a watch collector, I love a brand of watches that has three labels under them. I may purchase 10 watches a year. My watch collection can come out of nowhere, I am not a flashy guy at all but I love my brand of watches.

Your Portfolio

I have to admit that the brand that I love is not an expensive brand. However, some would say that they are expenses to them. I would say it is all relative, price and value is not an issue to a person who has passion for what he/she has passion for.

Now I am really thinking, how I can get you to start thinking about that pleasant feeling you get from collectibles or items you accumulate because the objects represent something that you value or serve as a way to connect with others.

I have this client who makes and collects quilts, it reminded me of my mother. As a kid I would sit with her at the sewing machine as she would create quilts to sell on request. She did it more as a hobby than as a business. She enjoyed making them, actually a few of her friends would also make them and exchanged them with each.

Now my head is spinning, all kinds of thoughts running through my mind. My business partner Mr. Funn is also a collector, I cannot begin to describe his collection of dolls, action figures, books and magazines.

I also remember when I got my first apartment I tried to have a passion for music. I began collecting vinyl records at the time. It was a little pricey, but it is worth it. When I bought my first record player and my first vinyl, it was a special moment for me.

Before I knew it, I was a part of some club sending me records every month and asking for payment. That ended that experiment with music.

I worked in the radio business for 15 plus years. Let me restate that, I was a host of a financial talk show on radio for over 15 years. I had nothing at all to do with the music side.

However, I had a colleague that is still one of the greatest evening drive time DJs. He had back in 1999 one of the largest collections of sneakers anywhere in the US.

That has been something that I watched grow and become a major thing for men and women of all ages. Mind-blowing culture to see grow and expand, I wanted to know what drives this type of commitment. I will share with you what I discovered.

The most common reason people collect sneakers is that they love the sneaker culture. They love the designs, colors, and materials that make different shoes. If you pick up a few pairs of limited-edition sneakers, it's easy to peg you as a collector.

Collecting sneakers is also a great way to be a part of the sneaker community. There are tons of events that are hosted all over the world, bringing together people who love sneakers.

The rush of finding a rare pair of limited-edition sneakers is real. It's like treasure hunting, and the thrill of the hunt can be addictive. But what happens when your search for limited edition sneakers goes wrong?

It can be hard to predict how many pairs of a particular model will be available. It's also hard to know when these sneakers will be released. It's not uncommon to find yourself stuck in a mad dash to the store when you're hoping to score a pair of sneakers.

For every person who loves collecting sneakers, there are probably two other people who hate it. And for good reason. Sneaker collecting is an investment, (What?) and not all investments are created equal. It's not uncommon for a pair of Air Jordan's to sell for $20,000 or more.

For sneaker collectors just starting, the high price tags of coveted sneakers can be daunting. You might have to spend a lot of money on a few pairs of shoes just to get started or settle for a lower-end version of the shoes you want—all in the hopes that one day you'll be able to sell them for a profit.

Collecting is a great way to find rare sneakers. But it's also a great way to spend a lot of money. The best way to build your dream shoe collection is by picking up a few rare pairs here and there. But if you're hoping to amass an awe-inspiring collection of rare sneakers, you'll need a lot of money.

You want to make sure you have a budget set aside for collecting. You'll also want to make sure you have a few places you frequent, such as auctions, eBay, and Amazon, where you can look for rare sneakers.

If you're looking to build a collection of rare sneakers, you'll want to check out some of the most collected brands. While every brand has limited-edition sneakers, these are the ones most likely to hold their value.

These brands are most likely to be featured in online auctions. Collecting Nike, Jordan, and Adidas sneakers is a great way to start your collection, but if you're hoping to collect rare sneakers, you might want to consider branching out.

Collecting sneakers is a great hobby. It's a fun way to be a part of the sneaker community and a great way to show off your love for sneakers. But, remember, you could collect sneakers for yourself and the love of creating a collection.

These stories I hope opened your eyes to the concept of great hobbies and the collection of goods. What I really hope is that you were kicked in the mouth, knocked down to the floor, hit in the eye. Do I have your attention yet?

Before I go into portfolio I really want you to understand that you have what it will take of you inside you already. Too often you are using your gift and knowledge in every area of your life except your financial future and wealth creation.

This is the thing I practice that helps me create a standard of information and solutions for my clients and now my readers. It's called the habit of collection, it is nothing more than a process of capturing everything on your mind and putting it into separate "baskets."

It has been one of the best personal changes I've ever made. In overwhelmingly busy times, the habits keep me sane, and in other times, it helps me to stay in an optimal mental state of creativity and relaxation.

Your Portfolio

For you this is all about getting every single open loop, unfinished project, task, or other incomplete action off of your mind and into some type of system that allows you to have control. This concept probably isn't new to you.

You already have an email inbox and maybe a physical inbox on your desk. These are perfect examples of you organizing on purpose. The important habit that most people don't implement, however, is the collection of 100% of the open loops and disconnects in your life into your inboxes and off of your mind.

The Portfolio

When you start considering creating your portfolio, you should understand that the habit, the concept, the purpose and the value thinking is already present with you. Will you continue to use it as your day to day stuff, maintaining the awesome job that you have, getting your 3% match?

Now that you have seen the make-up of different collections of things, let's look at the reason you are reading this book. Wealth creation!

The decision to start investing for your future is the first of many steps you will take on your investment journey. What comes next is constructing a robust investment portfolio that supports your financial goals and objectives.

In this chapter I am aiming to cover everything you need to know about creating a good investment portfolio.

First, understand that an investment portfolio or a financial portfolio is a basket of financial assets that may include stocks, bonds, money market instruments, cash and cash equivalents, commodities, etc.

You should aim for significant returns by mixing these investment options in a way that best reflects your financial goals and risk appetite. I talked about it in the last chapter.

Without an investment portfolio in place, you might be unprepared for several major milestones in your life. A portfolio with an appropriate (diversified) mix of investments not only helps to protect your invested capital but also allows you to position it in a way that it has the potential to earn desirable returns.

In the long term, this will allow you to achieve your various financial goals, such as planning for your retirement, wealth creation, etc.

By developing an investment portfolio that centers around income securities, one can supplement your income in the future. For instance, when you dedicate a fraction of assets to dividend-paying stocks, you may create a stable income stream.

Stock dividends are not usually assured but certain companies make uninterrupted payments over time. You can also invest in bonds to generate income, as these fixed-income securities generally make regular interest payments over the tenure of the investment.

Your Portfolio

Having a financial portfolio by itself is not enough. You must judiciously allocate your capital to reap the benefits of being exposed to the risk of the financial markets.

By creating a diversified financial portfolio that is spread across various investment categories, you can reap the benefits of diversification. Diversification across multiple asset classes helps to protect your capital if one sector of the financial market does not perform well. Go back to "The Mindset" for a refresher

The components of an investment portfolio consist of various securities known as asset classes. You must ensure that your portfolio has a good mix of assets to stimulate capital growth with controlled or limited risk. An investment portfolio usually has the following components:

Stocks

Stocks are one of the most common components of an investment portfolio. They are a representation of the total share capital of a given company traded over the stock exchanges.

Thus, if you are a shareholder, it means that you own a stake in the company. The size of the ownership stake is determined by the number of shares an individual owns.

Bonds

Bonds are investment securities that allow you to lend money to the government, an agency, or a company for a fixed period of time in lieu of regular interest payments. Bonds have a fixed maturity date, post which the principal amount is returned to you with interest. As compared to stocks, bonds are comparatively less risky but also offer lower potential returns.

Alternate investment options

An investment portfolio can also contain alternate investments, i.e. assets whose value can grow and multiply, such as oil, real estate, gold, etc. Usually, alternate investment options are not as widely traded as traditional investments such as bonds and stocks.

Here are the different types of portfolios.

Remember how I broke down strategies? There are different types of financial portfolios depending on the strategies used for investment. Some of these are:

1. Growth portfolio

The primary aim of a growth portfolio is to promote growth by undertaking more significant risks, including investing in growing companies. These portfolios usually offer significant potential rewards and concurrent higher risks both. Growth portfolios often invest in younger companies that have greater potential for growth than larger, well-established firms.

2. Value portfolio

Under these, you would buy cheap assets by taking advantage of their low valuations. These portfolios are especially useful during challenging economic conditions when several investments and businesses struggle to survive and stay afloat.

You should search for companies that have profit potential but are currently priced below their fair market value. In short, value investing focuses on finding good bargains in the market.

3. Income portfolio

An income portfolio is more focused on obtaining regular income from investment options rather than focusing on potential capital gains.

For instance, you might consider buying a stock based on its historic dividend payouts rather than its historic price appreciation. Moreover, fixed-income assets typically provide regular income to you, making them ideal for those looking for stable returns.

Consider your risk appetite

Risk refers to the degree of uncertainty or potential financial loss that could arise due to the poor performance of the market or a particular asset class.

Risk appetite or risk tolerance, in simple terms, means how much you can afford to invest and how much you can stand to lose without being financially affected when the markets are volatile.

Broadly, you have three types of risk tolerance, namely low-risk, moderate risk, and high-risk. This is a tricky area to navigate and requires you to consider multiple factors such as the nature of your income, the number of dependents you have, your liquidity requirements, etc., to conclude where you fall on the risk spectrum.

If you need your capital in a few years and can't stomach the ups and downs in the market, you have a low-risk tolerance. On the other hand, if you don't need your money for a long time, say 15-20+ years, you can probably tolerate more volatility and the ups and downs of the market.

You would have enough time to wait out a drop in your investment value, if any, before the market bounces back. Clearly, in this case, you have a high-risk tolerance.

You should always consider the investment horizon when building your financial portfolio. Everyone has a different risk appetite based on their life situations and financial goals.

For instance, a college graduate could probably invest aggressively for a financially secure future as time is on his/her side.

Meanwhile, a 55-year-old individual who is nearing retirement might not be able to risk a portfolio drop and will, thus, have a far more conservative investment portfolio.

If you have a high-risk tolerance, you might consider looking at high risk-reward investment avenues such as equity mutual funds# or stocks that have the potential to offer inflation-beating returns in the long run. Keep in mind that they are subject to market risk but this is a trade-off you should be willing to accept.

On the contrary, if you think you want to lower the risk associated with investing in equities and play it relatively safer, you may consider investing in fixed-income securities such as debt mutual funds, recurring deposits, fixed deposits, etc.

Remember, safety equals low to moderate returns, so the returns on fixed-income assets will not be the same as equities, as the former are less volatile.

Determine your current financial position. This includes listing down assets such as stocks, mutual funds, bonds, cash, property, etc., and liabilities such as debt, credit card dues, student loan debt, etc.

This balance sheet will give you a clearer idea of your net worth and will also act as a benchmark for building your financial future.

Buy a house

The next step in building your financial portfolio is to save for the down payment to purchase a house. By owning a house, you convert your rent liability into an asset. To sweeten the deal, the principal amount on home loans is eligible for tax deduction.

Build a Protection Fund

You must build a protection fund that has at least six months' worth of living expenses to cover any unexpected events such as job loss, surprise home repairs, medical emergencies, etc. Your protection fund should be able to cover the following expenses:

Some of the best investment options to park your protection funds are overnight funds, liquid mutual funds, savings accounts, money market instruments, etc. Remember, the primary objective of your protection fund is safety and liquidity and not returns.

Look for other investment opportunities

After completing the steps mentioned above, consider additional investment opportunities such as bonds, stocks, mutual funds, ETFs (exchange-traded funds), certificates of deposit (CD), etc. You can also opt for a financial advisor to guide you on your investment journey and help you chart the best way forward.

Invest in yourself

If you are planning to stand out to potential employers, or improve your professional skills, or even start your own business, invest in yourself by undertaking valuable educational courses.

This will enable you to increase your earning potential and accelerate your financial plans. Several colleges and universities offer various professional certification programs that you can take advantage of.

Save for your child's future

Every parent wants to ensure the best for their child, which includes providing them with good educational opportunities. However, with the costs associated with higher education growing at a rapid pace, it's important to invest in your child's future by building an educational corpus for them.

Stay on course

By completing all these steps, you will have successfully laid the foundation for a successful financial future. The key to success is making informed decisions and sticking to your financial plan.

Remember, wealth creation is a regular effort made by small and disciplined choices. You can also seek the help of a financial advisor who will help to build a financial portfolio for you to aid you on your journey.

Reduces the impact of market volatility

A diversified investment portfolio helps minimize the overall risk associated with the portfolio. As investments are made across varying asset classes and categories, the overall impact of market volatility tends to decrease.

By choosing different investment options such as mutual funds, ETFs, fixed deposits, etc., you can enjoy the unique features of each instrument and mitigate risk.

For instance, by investing in fixed deposits, an investor can enjoy fixed returns at lower risk, but with equity mutual funds, they have the potential to earn relatively higher returns as the risk is equally high.

Preserving capital is the basic criterion for several investors. You who have just started investing prefer to take risk while those that are on the verge of retirement prefer stability.

Here's where portfolio diversification can help you achieve your goals. Diversification allows you to achieve your investment goals by limiting exposure to particular investments.

At the core of a diversified portfolio are investment options that react to specific economic conditions. While you having diversified your portfolio won't achieve abnormally high returns as opposed to one owning a single, high-flying stock, you will also not suffer the ups and downs in the market like the latter.

In short, you will generate weighted average returns on your underlying securities, but would also not be fully exposed to the volatility associated with a particular security.

One of the biggest advantages of diversifying a portfolio is that it offers peace of mind to you. When the total corpus is divided among a variety of asset classes and categories, you will not be stressed about the performance of the portfolio.

Achieving your long-term financial goals requires balancing risks against rewards. While there are several ways to invest, there's no 'one-size-fits-all' approach to investing.

So, choose the right mix of investments for your portfolio and make sure to rebalance and monitor your financial choices periodically. Remember, your investments should align with your financial goals, risk appetite, and investment horizon.

Happy investing!

Chapter Seven

Products

An investment product is a product offered to investors based on an underlying security or group of securities that is purchased with the expectation of earning a favorable return. Investment products are based on a wide range of underlying securities and encompass a broad range of investment objectives.

Understanding Investment Products

Investment product is the umbrella term for all the stocks, bonds, options, derivatives and other financial instruments that you put money into in hopes of earning profits.

The types of investment products available for individual and institutional investors can differ significantly but the basic profit motive is behind all of them.

A wide range of investment products exist within the investment universe to help you meet short-term and long-term investment goals. Overall, you purchase investment products for your capital appreciation potential and income paying distributions.

Capital appreciation and income distribution are two standard classifications for investment products. Some investment products are purchased by you primarily for their potential to increase or appreciate in value over time given specific growth factors. Other investment products may have an additional income paying component. Fixed income investments such as bonds and commingled bond funds offer investors the opportunity to purchase an asset that may increase in value while also paying out fixed interest payments or capital distributions.

Other income paying investment products include dividend-paying equities, real estate investment trusts and master limited partnerships. Modern portfolio theory suggests that you have a diversified portfolio of investments including a variety of investment products to obtain an optimal risk-return reward for their investments.

Within the investment market, investment products can be structured in various ways. Thus, you have a wide variety of options in addition to buying an investment product focused on the movement of a single security. Structured investment products can include mutual funds, exchange traded funds, money market funds, annuities and more.

Below are some basic examples of investment products offered in the investment universe.

Stocks

Stock investments represent equity ownership in a publicly traded company. Companies issue stock as part of a capital raising regime which funds the operations of the company.

Stock investments have varying growth prospects and are typically analyzed based on characteristics such as estimated future earnings and price-to-earnings ratios. Stocks can be classified in various categories and may also offer dividends adding an income payout component to the investment.

Bonds

Bonds are one of the most well-known fixed income investment products. They can be offered by governments or corporations looking to raise capital. Bonds pay you interest in the form of coupon payments and offer full principal repayment at maturity.

You can also invest in bond funds which include a portfolio of bonds managed by a portfolio manager for various objectives. Bonds and bond funds are typically classified by a credit rating which offers insight on their capital structure and ability to make timely payments.

Derivatives

Derivatives are investment products that are offered based on the movement of a specified underlying asset. Put or call options on stocks and futures based on the movement of commodities prices are a few of the market's leading derivative investment products.

There are also futures and customized investment products that allow you to speculate on price movements or move risk between parties. Derivatives are complex investment products, so a certain level of market knowledge and experience is required

Products

The main categories of investment products are:

Stock
Bonds
Mutual Funds and ETFs
Insurance Products such as Variable Annuities (I will cover these in the next chapter)

Selecting Investment Products

By now you should have a great idea of what type of strategy you want to employ around your investment goals. If you have not, please move in that direction before moving forward.

This content is for the book "The Mindset" Write down the financial goals that you want to establish, create a strategy for each one of them that allows you to level up.

Here is an example of what I mean about establishing a strategy that would allow you to level up on whatever your financial goals are. Many years ago I opened up a bank account and started a certificate of deposit (CD) at that bank.

I realized that each month I will make a $88 payment towards a $1000 CD over the course of one year and each year I have a 10 day period for which I will be able to cash in or reassign that CD.

The goal was to use what most of us call the latter approach, which is you open up the CD and you begin to reach your goals

92

and create another level that each step you build and go to the next step and you continue that process.

At this stage of your wealth creation what you want to do is the identical thing, you want to begin to process regardless of how small or large you want to create a process with the goals in mind of each time you will level up, you will go higher.

When we are talking about stocks and stock ownership we're looking at products that will provide us dividend payments, these dividend payments that we will reinvest, it becomes that compounding effect.

So, as you select stocks and create your strategy towards managing and reaching your financial goals, wealth creation with each opportunity should give you the ability to level up.

You will devise a strategy for choosing investments appropriate for each of your investment goals, you've taken a major step toward meeting them. Please do not take this moment likely, this really can be your time that the cycle of generational wealth is changing to your favor.

Whether you decide to use an investment professional or not, it's important to understand what your investment choices are and how different types of investments put your money to work.

It's equally important to understand yourself as an investor, we just talked about this. That's because a portfolio that's right for someone else may not be best for you.

Products

Some factors that can make a difference in your investment selection are your goals, or what you want to accomplish by investing, and the time frames for meeting those goals. It's also important to have a handle on your attitude toward risk, or what's called your risk tolerance.

Let me be clear, no single approach to choosing investments will work for everyone or will be right for every situation. But here are a few tried-and-true rules for sound investment selection.

Know what you own. Focus on investments that are easy for you to evaluate and give you access to reliable information about them.

Regulators require that certain information be disclosed to you through documents such as offering circulars, mutual fund prospectuses, and corporate filings for stock issued by public companies that trade on the major stock markets.

In addition, you can find a wealth of real-time and historical market data for stocks, bonds, mutual funds, and other securities online.

Assess liquidity. Make sure there is a market to trade your investments. Highly liquid investments are easy to buy and sell, either through a brokerage account or in some cases directly from the issuer.

Thinly traded stocks or securities that aren't listed on a national securities exchange tend to be less liquid -- and are rarely a good idea for most investors seasoned or not seasoned.

Likewise, exercise caution when considering securities such as non-traded REITs that may be illiquid -- meaning you can't cash out of them even if you really need to -- for long periods of time.

Know the true cost. Have a clear understanding of any costs, sales charges, and fees involved with buying and selling investment products, including whether there are penalties or additional fees for selling your investment within a certain time frame.

Understanding risk is key. When you select any investment product, it's vital to understand that all investments carry some level of risk. Stocks, bonds, mutual funds, and exchange-traded funds (ETFs) can lose value -- even all their value -- if market conditions sour.

Even conservative, insured investments, such as certificates of deposit (CDs) issued by a bank or credit union, come with inflation risk; they may not earn enough over time to keep pace with the increasing cost of living. Whatever investment you're considering, be sure you know how it can make or lose money before you buy.

Risk is uncertainty with respect to your investments that has the potential to negatively affect your financial welfare. For example, your investment value might rise or fall because of market conditions (market risk) the first and second quarter of 2022 is evidence.

Corporate decisions, such as whether to expand into a new area of business or merge with another company, can also affect the value of your investments (business risk). If you own an international investment, events within that country can affect your investment (political risk and currency risk, to name two).

There are other types of risk to consider. How easy or hard it is to cash out of an investment when you need to is called liquidity risk.

Another risk factor is tied to how many or how few investments you hold. Generally speaking, the more financial eggs you have in one basket (say, all your money in a single stock), the greater risk you take (concentration risk).

Time frames and investment selection

For every financial goal you set, think about the time frame in which you might need the money you have invested. For near-term goals, you'll want to consider moving some or all of your portfolio into liquid, lower-volatility investments such as short-term bonds, certificates of deposit, and cash.

For longer-term goals, stocks and mutual funds that invest in stocks have the potential to provide higher returns. Based on historical data, holding a broad portfolio of stocks over an extended period of time (for instance, a large-cap portfolio like the S&P 500 over a 20-year period) significantly reduces your chances of losing your principal.

However, the historical data should not mislead you into thinking that there is no risk in investing in stocks over a long period of time.

You are an investor now and you should consider how realistic it will be for you to ride out the ups and downs of the market over the long term.

Will you have to sell stocks during an economic downturn to fill the gap caused by a job loss? Will you sell investments to pay for medical care or a child's college education?

Predictable and unpredictable life events might make it difficult for you to stay invested in stocks over an extended period of time. This is why I am asking you to consider every aspect.

The bottom line: At every stage of your investing life, the more carefully you plan and the more informed the investment decisions you make, the better the chances you'll have of meeting all of your investment goals and achieving a secure financial future.

Investing in the stock market has historically been one of the most important pathways to financial success. As you dive into researching stocks, you'll often hear them discussed with reference to different categories of stocks and different classifications.

Products

Here are the major types of stocks you should know.

Common stock
Preferred stock
Large-cap stocks
Mid-cap stocks
Small-cap stocks
Domestic stock
International stocks
Growth stocks
Value stocks
IPO stocks
Dividend stocks

Non-dividend stocks
Income stocks
Cyclical stocks
Non-cyclical stocks
Safe stocks
ESG stocks
Blue chip stocks
Penny stocks
Common stock
Preferred stock

Most stocks that people invest in are common stock. Common stock represents partial ownership in a company, with shareholders getting the right to receive a proportional share of the value of any remaining assets if the company gets dissolved.

Common stock gives shareholders theoretically unlimited upside potential, but they also risk losing everything if the company fails without having any assets left over.

Preferred stock works differently, as it gives shareholders a preference over common shareholders to get back a certain amount of money if the company dissolves. Preferred shareholders also have the right to receive dividend payments before common shareholders do.

The net result is that preferred stock as an investment often more closely resembles fixed-income bond investments than regular common stock. Often, a company will offer only common stock. This makes sense, as that is what shareholders most often seek to buy.

Large-cap, mid-cap, and small-cap stocks

Stocks also get categorized by the total worth of all their shares, which is called market capitalization. Companies with the biggest market capitalizations are called large-cap stocks, with mid-cap and small-cap stocks representing successively smaller companies.

There's no precise line that separates these categories from each other. However, one often-used rule is that stocks with market capitalizations of $10 billion or more are treated as large-caps, with stocks having market caps between $2 billion and $10 billion qualifying as mid-caps and stocks with market caps below $2 billion getting treated as small-cap stocks.

Large-cap stocks are generally considered safer and more conservative as investments, while mid-caps and small caps have greater capacity for future growth but are riskier.

However, just because two companies fall into the same category here doesn't mean they have anything else in common as investments or that they'll perform in similar ways in the future.

Make your portfolio reflect your best vision for our future.

Domestic stocks and international stocks

You can categorize stocks by where they're located. For purposes of distinguishing domestic U.S. stocks from international stocks, most investors look at the location of the company's official headquarters.

However, it's important to understand that a stock's geographical category doesn't necessarily correspond to where the company gets its sales. Philip Morris International (NYSE:PM) is a great example, as its headquarters are in the U.S., but it sells its tobacco and other products exclusively outside the country.

Especially among large multinational corporations, it can be hard to tell from business operations and financial metrics whether a company is truly domestic or international.

Growth stocks and value stocks

Another categorization method distinguishes between two popular investment methods. Growth investors tend to look for companies that are seeing their sales and profits rise quickly.

Value investors look for companies whose shares are inexpensive, whether relative to their peers or to their own past stock price.

Growth stocks tend to have higher risk levels, but the potential returns can be extremely attractive. Successful growth stocks have businesses that tap into strong and rising demand among customers, especially in connection with longer-term trends throughout society that support the use of their products and services.

Competition can be fierce, though, and if rivals disrupt a growth stock's business, it can fall from favor quickly. Sometimes, even just a growth slowdown is enough to send prices sharply lower, as investors fear that long-term growth potential is waning.

Value stocks, on the other hand, are seen as being more conservative investments. They're often mature, well-known companies that have already grown into industry leaders and therefore don't have as much room left to expand further. Yet with reliable business models that have stood the test of time, they can be good choices for those seeking more price stability while still getting some of the positives of exposure to stocks.

IPO stocks

IPO stocks are stocks of companies that have recently gone public through an initial public offering. IPOs often generate a lot of excitement among investors looking to get in on the ground floor of a promising business concept.

But they can also be volatile, especially when there's disagreement within the investment community about their prospects for growth and profit. A stock generally retains its status as an IPO stock for at least a year and for as long as two to four years after it becomes public.

Products

Dividend stocks and non-dividend stocks

Many stocks make dividend payments to their shareholders on a regular basis. Dividends provide valuable income for you, and that makes dividend stocks highly sought after among certain investment circles. Technically, paying even $0.01 per share qualifies a company as a dividend stock.

However, stocks don't have to pay dividends. Non-dividend stocks can still be strong investments if their prices rise over time. Some of the biggest companies in the world don't pay dividends, although the trend in recent years has been toward more stocks making dividend payouts to their shareholders.

Income stocks

Income stocks are another name for dividend stocks, as the income that most stocks pay out comes in the form of dividends. However, income stocks also refer to shares of companies that have more mature business models and have relatively fewer long-term opportunities for growth.

Ideal for conservative investors who need to draw cash from their investment portfolios right now, income stocks are a favorite among those in or nearing retirement.

Cyclical stocks and non-cyclical stocks

National economies tend to follow cycles of expansion and contraction, with periods of prosperity and recession. Certain businesses have greater exposure to broad business cycles, and you therefore refer to them as cyclical stocks.

Cyclical stocks include shares of companies in industries like manufacturing, travel, and luxury goods, because an economic downturn can take away customers' ability to make major purchases quickly. When economies are strong, however, a rush of demand can make these companies rebound sharply.

By contrast, non-cyclical stocks, also known as secular or defensive stocks, don't have those big swings in demand. An example would be grocery store chains, because no matter how good or bad the economy is, people still have to eat. Non-cyclical stocks tend to perform better during market downturns, while cyclical stocks often outperform during strong bull markets.

Safe stocks

Safe stocks are stocks whose share prices make relatively small movements up and down compared with the overall stock market. Also known as low-volatility stocks, safe stocks typically operate in industries that aren't as sensitive to changing economic conditions. They often pay dividends as well, and that income can offset falling share prices during tough times.

Stock market sectors

You'll often see stocks broken down by the type of business they're in. The basic categories most often used include stock market sectors. This is an excellent way for you to target various

Products

sectors and build unique portfolios. Understanding different categories of stocks is key to building a strong portfolio.

•Communication Services -- telephone, internet, media, and entertainment companies

•Consumer Discretionary -- retailers, automakers, and hotel and restaurant companies

•Consumer Staples -- food, beverage, tobacco, and household and personal products companies

•Energy -- oil and gas exploration and production companies, pipeline providers, and gas station operators

•Financial -- banks, mortgage finance specialists, and insurance and brokerage companies

•Healthcare -- health insurers, drug and biotech companies, and medical device makers

•Industrial -- airline, aerospace and defense, construction, logistics, machinery, and railroad companies

•Materials -- mining, forest products, construction materials, packaging, and chemical companies

•Real Estate -- real estate investment trusts and real estate management and development companies

•Technology -- hardware, software, semiconductor, communications equipment, and IT services companies

•Utilities -- electric, natural gas, water, renewable energy, and multi-product utility companies

•Stock Exchanges – Exchanges are where you buy and sell shares of stock.

•Stock Market Indexes - Indexes illustrate stock prices for a variety of companies across industries.

ESG investing

ESG Investing refers to an investment philosophy that puts emphasis on environmental, social, and governance concerns. Rather than focusing entirely on whether a company generates profit and is growing its revenue over time, ESG principles consider other collateral impacts on the environment, company employees, customers, and shareholder rights.

Tied to ESG's governing rules is socially responsible investing, or SRI. Investors using SRI screen out stocks of companies that don't match up to their most important values.

However, ESG investing has a more positive element in that rather than just excluding companies that fail key tests, it actively encourages investing in the companies that do things the best. With evidence showing that a clear commitment to ESG principles can improve investing returns, there's a lot of interest in the area.

Blue chip stocks and penny stocks

Finally, there are stock categories that make judgments based on perceived quality. Blue chip stocks tend to be the cream of the crop in the business world, featuring companies that lead their respective industries and have gained strong reputations.

They typically don't provide the absolute highest returns, but their stability makes them favorites among investors with lower tolerance for risk.

Products

By contrast, penny stocks are low-quality companies whose stock prices are extremely inexpensive, typically less than $1 per share. With dangerously speculative business models, penny stocks are prone to schemes that can drain your entire investment. It's important to know about the dangers of penny stocks.

Here is a habit exercise that will allow you to create wealth with a direct focus. It has nothing to do with talent or skills or luck for that matter just being intentional.

Each week follow the guide on the next page, each week you purchase at least the number of shares of the type of stocks for that week. You will be creating your personal portfolio of stocks that you own.

These stocks are for long term purposes, an exercise that you are creating to create a habit that carries value for you in your financial future. You do not have to do this. "LOL"

Create your stock purchase schedule. No minimum or maximum price.

Common stock	Buy Minimum 1 Share Week 1 & 22, 43
Preferred stock	Buy Minimum 2 Share Week 2 & 23, 44
Large-cap stocks	Buy Minimum 3 Share Week 3 & 24, 45
Mid-cap stocks	Buy Minimum 4 Share Week 4 & 25, 46
Small-cap stocks	Buy Minimum 5 Share Week 5 & 26, 47
Domestic stock	Buy Minimum 1 Share Week 6 & 27, 48
International stocks	Buy Minimum 2 Share Week 7 & 28
Growth stocks	Buy Minimum 3 Share Week 8 & 29, 49
Value stocks	Buy Minimum 4 Share Week 9 & 30
IPO stocks	Buy Minimum 5 Share Week 10 & 31
Dividend stocks	Buy Minimum 1 Share Week 11 & 32, 50
Non-dividend stocks	Buy Minimum 2 Share Week 12 & 33
Income stocks	Buy Minimum 3 Share Week 13 & 34, 51
Cyclical stocks	Buy Minimum 4 Share Week 14 & 35
Non-cyclical stocks	Buy Minimum 5 Share Week 15 & 36
Safe stocks	Buy Minimum 1 Share Week 16 & 37
ESG stocks	Buy Minimum 2 Share Week 17 & 38
Blue chip stocks	Buy Minimum 3 Share Week 18 & 39
Penny stocks	Buy Minimum 4 Share Week 19 & 40, 52
Common stocks	Buy Minimum 5 Share Week 20 & 41
Preferred stocks	Buy Minimum 1 Share Week 21 & 42

If by chance you decide to do this process, you should end up with a portfolio of 21 types of stocks and a total of over 100 shares of stocks.

The Takeaway

There are products like annuities that are contracts sold by insurance companies that make regular payments to you for a set period or for life. You invest an initial sum, and then the money is repaid to you in periodic installments, a process known as annuitizing. The payments typically consist of both principal and interest.

Income investing is often associated with older investors, often retired investors: Common financial wisdom often has portfolios shifting from growth to income as the owner ages. Still, as a wealth creator you can and should include some income producers in your portfolio - as a counterbalance to aggressive growth assets, if nothing else.

Generally speaking, the more risk you are willing to take or the longer you are willing to let your money work, the higher rate of return you will receive.

That said, the main purpose of building a portfolio and income investing is to produce cash flow with a reasonable amount of risk. Income-producing stocks, bonds, and other securities are meant to be the stable foundation of your portfolio. You can always diversify your risk further by investing in income-oriented exchange-traded funds (ETFs) and mutual funds.

Chapter Eight

Wealth Management

Your wealth—as measured by both possessions and money—should be managed in order to grow or to avoid losing value. Wealth management is the process of reviewing and making decisions about your wealth so you can achieve your financial goals.

A sound wealth strategy provides a road map for protecting and preserving your family's assets, or those of your business. Regardless of your income, estate planning is a vital part of your financial plan. Planning ahead can give you greater control, privacy, and security of your legacy.

If you stay on course and create wealth as you have learned through this series you will need services within the field of wealth management that may include investment, retirement, tax or estate planning.

Wealth management is the process of making decisions about your assets, sometimes with a wealth manager, trust me you cannot do this alone. This includes, but isn't limited to, financial investments, tax planning, estate planning and other financial matters.

The decision to use a wealth manager depends on your financial situation and goals, as well as your financial expertise.

If you're clear about your goals and confident in your ability to choose the products and strategies that will help you grow and protect your wealth, you may not need the help of a wealth manager.

Other advisors you work with on a regular basis—like your accountant or attorney—may also be able to provide insight into whether a wealth manager can help with your financial needs. I must share this story: I made an investment in a private start-up that netted a return of eight figures.

I called my tax guy and my accountant on advice to minimize taxes for this money before it was to be wired into my business account. What I discovered was neither one of my relationships had the knowledge to guide me in my new situation.

I needed the power of tax lawyers, accounting lawyers and estate lawyers. This was a new financial G.A.M.E. (Gaining Assets Manage Effectively), no disrespect to my old tax person and accountant, I outgrown their knowledge.

The goal of wealth management is to help you achieve financial security and grow and protect your wealth. Your goal is to grow and preserve your wealth over the long term.

Investment management. A wealth manager will work with you to develop an investment strategy tailored to your goals and risk tolerance.

If the manager is a licensed investment advisor, they may also select and manage investments on your behalf, often in exchange for an annual fee.

Financial planning. A wealth manager can help you develop a financial plan that includes saving, investing and spending goals.

The manager can also help you plan for retirement, saving for college and other major life events. These plans can be revisited periodically as your circumstances change.

Tax advice. A wealth manager can provide advice on how to structure your finances in a way that minimizes your tax liability. This is especially important if you own your own business or have multiple income streams.

Estate planning. A wealth manager can help you develop a plan for what will happen to your assets after your death. This may include creating a will or trust and designated beneficiaries.

However, if you run into questions you can't answer, or have needs that could benefit from input from a specialist, then a wealth manager could help you make informed decisions about your finances and provide guidance throughout the process.

When choosing a wealth manager, it's important to find a professional who is reputable and has the right licenses and expertise to give you sound guidance for your unique needs.

For example, some certifications you might look for include certified investment management analyst (CIMA), certified private wealth advisor (CPWA) and certified financial planner (CFP), among others.

Strategies used by wealth managers vary across the industry. On the investment side, some of the most common strategies include:

Asset allocation. The process of dividing an investment portfolio among different asset categories like stocks and bonds.

Diversification. A risk management technique that involves investing in a variety of assets to minimize the impact of losses in any one particular asset.

Rebalancing. The process of realigning a portfolio's assets to maintain the original risk/reward ratio when things shift.

Tax-loss harvesting. A strategy used to minimize capital gains taxes by selling securities that have experienced losses and replacing them with similar investments.

These are just a few of the strategies that wealth managers may use to help you reach your investing goals. The specific strategies employed will depend on your unique situation.

Wealth strategy plays an important role in safeguarding your family's wealth, avoiding unnecessary taxes, and ensuring that your legacy will continue.

You or your strategist will need to work with your attorney, tax advisor or accountant to design sophisticated, customized plans that can help you achieve a careful balance of control and flexibility, shaping your family's future while responding to its changing needs.

A large part of that is the following.

Evaluating insurance needs
Protecting your assets
Planning for taxes
Transferring wealth and gifting
Developing a family or business succession plan

One of your primary concerns may be accumulating sufficient assets to live a fulfilling and comfortable retirement. And, planning for the non-financial aspects and unknown contingencies that may arise during retirement is also important.

Whether you are near retirement, many years away, or living it now, your retirement goals will need objective guidance, monitoring and reviews of your progress.

Your Wealth Strategist could help you estimate your family members' current and future education costs. As well as evaluate tax-efficient savings options and suggest planning, trust, investments and insurance strategies to help make education goals a reality.

Protecting your wealth is as important as growing it. Appropriate insurance coverage is an integral part of any financial plan. As a risk management option, insurance can replace lost income due to disability or death, provide needed funds for estate taxes or help pay for long-term care, or help ensure continuity of business interests. A comprehensive insurance review can:

Help determine if your family or your business is appropriately covered

Identify coverage gaps and recommend new coverage where indicated

Reveal the need for updated beneficiary selections

Suggest future funding patterns based on longevity and likely performance

Modify existing coverage for cost effectiveness and maximum Return on Investment

Life insurance can play a versatile role in your overall wealth strategy. Life is unpredictable. How can you incorporate insurance planning into your overall wealth strategy plan?

I would like to introduce you to Dr. C. W. Copeland the author of two powerful life changing books as well as an expert in Life Insurance and Annuities to protect your financial future. His books are listed below:

- Financial Planning for Poor People: Financial Professionals Guide to Working with Low-Income to Middle-Income Individuals this book aims to share sound financial principles; so, that you know what "right" looks like

- The Personal Economic Model this book brings a foundational understanding to managing the multitude of financial decisions one must make during their lifetime.

A trust is a powerful estate planning tool that can ensure that your wishes are carried out at the end of your life. This legal solution can also make the process of transferring your property easier for your loved ones.

You don't have to have millions in the bank for a trust to effectively help you plan for the future. Before you can determine what type of trust is best for you, you should speak with knowledgeable attorneys.

There are many benefits of including a trust in your estate plan. A living trust not only has the potential to ensure your final wishes are met, but it can also assist with your financial needs until the end of your life.

A trust can provide flexibility, giving you options on how your property, including your house and savings, is used both during and after your life. Many people don't know, but a trust can avoid the need for a guardianship and conservatorship when someone loses capacity.

A properly created trust can also help protect your property from creditors. A trust that is drafted and funded correctly will enable your beneficiaries to avoid probate court after your death.

Wealth Management

Without the correct type of trust, your beneficiaries will be required to go through the probate court process to transfer ownership of assets from you to them.

During the probate court process, creditors can come after the assets in your estate to pay your bills before your beneficiaries receive their inheritance.

When you pass, your trust becomes the owner of your property until the trust document determines it is time to distribute your belongings to the intended beneficiary.

Of course, trusts are not the right choice for everybody. An experienced trust lawyer can help you decide if a trust would be beneficial for you during the planning process.

While there are multiple types of trusts, one that is frequently used is a revocable living trust. The person creating the trust can be the trustee (manager of the trust) for this type of trust.

As the trustee, you can make changes during the course of your life and when you pass away, the trust operates similarly to a will. A revocable living trust distributes your property held by the trust to your beneficiaries once you pass.

The most common type of trust is an asset protection trust. When this type of trust is drafted correctly, you can make changes to the trust throughout your life, like a revocable living trust.

The biggest advantages of this trust are that it can protect your hard-earned life savings from creditors, lawsuits, and future medical costs (including the high cost of long-term care).

It can assist with the qualification for benefits to help you pay for care as you age. If you are worried about running out of money during your life, come and talk with our team about an asset protection trust.

Some trusts are not related to the distribution of property at all. For example, a special needs trust can set aside money for a child who will need specialized care for the remainder of their life. Trusts can also set aside funds for anything from nursing home expenses to the care of a beloved pet. FRFR

Many people pass away without a trust in place. While some have a will to rely on, others have no estate plan whatsoever. As a wealth creator you must work to preserve at all times.

Without a trust, your family must go through the probate court process, which can be time-consuming and costly. In most cases, probate could add months to the process of distributing your belongings to your heirs.

There are also potential tax consequences that come with not using a trust. Certain transfers to a trust during the course of your life could limit the tax liability your family faces once you pass.

Having knowledgeable attorneys can explain your options for limiting tax liability and help choose an effective strategy for your personal situation.

Trusts are complex but useful tools in an estate plan. Due to their strict requirements, a mistake or omission in crafting these documents can easily make them worthless.

To protect your rights and ensure that your future wishes will be respected, never attempt to create a trust on your own.

As I wrap this book up, I am realizing that there is another book for this series. In addition to a book a workbook with some advice from some people who are already a part of the 4% of the wealthy.

The closer I can place you in the space of wealth creation, I know the majority of you will get it and do something with this amazing information.

Everything about what you are seeking to do is a big financial moment where a do-over isn't possible, it can't hurt to consult with a wealth management professional who offers not just the knowledge but the experience, the tools, and the objective viewpoint you need to make shrewd moves.

It is a huge responsibility managing assets in a way that grows wealth while minimizing risk and it doesn't just require expertise and tooling, it also requires one very precious commodity: Time.

Time has to be spent acquiring assets, more time has to be spent researching the best strategies for managing those assets, and even more time has to be spent executing these strategies.

And these things don't just happen one time. Successful wealth management is all about consistency and repetition.

Listen carefully to me please, if you don't have the time, or simply aren't willing to spend the time required, to thoughtfully manage your wealth — the truth is that it's probably not going to happen. And the longer you delay crucial financial planning, the worse your results will be when you're finally forced to face it.

I kid you not, if wealth management keeps getting postponed in your household, wealth management services may be the way to go. You are constantly worried about your finances. You have long-term and short-term financial goals.

The more you manage to invest each month, the faster you can achieve your short-term and long-term financial goals. While you sweat to earn more, your money can sweat for you too.

This is not a get rich quick process if you have read the entire series I want you to know that I see your commitment.

Most important here is that you recognize your commitment to yourself and the commitment to your financial future. Your decision to trust the process and the effect of time on investing is powerful.

Investing can seem like a very risky, complex and fast-moving process. Right?

Wealth Management

With endless combinations of investment vehicles to choose from, it can be difficult to take your first step as wealth creator— especially with the knowledge that all investments carry the risk of losing some or all of your money. So why bother?

Well I will tell you why there are many compelling reasons to make investing a part of your overall financial plan. Investing can help preserve your wealth by overcoming the effects of inflation.

It will help you save for long-term goals (such as retirement or your children's education) and it can even generate income. So how can you get past all the negatives associated with investing and make it work for you? A helpful first step is to realize that, the younger you are as a wealth creator you have time on your side.

I might as well deal with this again and in fact I am going to touch on a number of areas that I have covered in this series to remind you of your mission.

We've all heard the stories (or seen the infomercials, or bought the e-book or got it for free) about those people who took a chance on a risky investment and by some stroke of luck woke up the next day as millionaires.

It's so easy to be drawn to "get rich quick" stories because we all secretly wish we could be the stars of those tales. Those success stories help establish the myth that being a successful wealth creator is a lot like being a hotshot gambler—

That you need to risk it all to get a worthwhile reward, and that some people are born with the innate ability to predict the market, make the right moves, buy and sell at the exact right time, and strike it rich. We can only wish so…

The truth is that serious investing requires a lot of time. There's an entire education behind active trading. If you were to invest into the stock market without any prior research, you might as well be playing the lottery.

Educating yourself about the stock market is no simple task and it requires ongoing research. It is not only about you understanding the way economies and global marketplaces work—it's also about staying up to date on what's happening in our world. Environment, technology, politics and culture all have the ability to influence economic forces.

Beyond understanding those interactions, as a smart wealth creator you also keep very close tabs on the industries and companies you invest in by monitoring things like performance, governance, public opinion and industry trends.

Now, imagine all that data changing and updating daily; suddenly, it's clear why it can—and should—take so much time to make educated investment decisions.

When you acknowledge that preparation takes an incredible amount of time, it minimizes the role that luck plays in investing. Suddenly it's less about taking a gamble and more about making calculated and educated decisions, which is a good thing—it means that investing is something you can practice, explore and ultimately improve on, over time.

For every investing success story, there's an accompanying horror story. This myth comes in different flavors—acting on bad advice, losing every last dime, and getting taken advantage of by an evil or incompetent financial advisor are just some of the common scripts.

This myth perpetuates the idea that investing is so scary and so unpredictable that it's simply not worth the risk.

It can be tricky trying to separate this myth from the truth, because risk and loss are both very real outcomes of investing. No investment is ever guaranteed, meaning your invested money is never absolutely safe.

Some investment types may be safer than others, but the risk of losing your money is ever-present.

After making smart, thoroughly researched investment choices, your next best protection against risk and volatility is the amount of time you have for your investment to mature.

The narrower your investment time frame, the more vulnerable you are to sudden and often unpredictable changes in the market. By contrast, if your investment is long term (think decades), day-to-day changes suddenly hold less influence.

Plus, there is time to recover from market declines; the same cannot always be said for short-term investments. Please understand the difference here. Remember, you heard this before, change the narrative.

Yet another investment myth is that it's impossible to find a combination of investment products within your risk tolerance level that will result in a high yield. In other words, playing it safe with your investments means measly returns.

Do you remember learning about compound interest?

Time happens to be compound interest's best buddy. Together, they can really put your money to work for you. This is especially important to note for long-term savings goals (retirement is a good example).

Even products with a relatively low expected yield can accumulate a lot of wealth over long periods of time, so do not get discouraged by low interest rates on investment products.

Look for opportunities to maximize the effect of compound interest, such as reinvesting your dividends or refraining from cashing out your investment early.

As you can see, time plays a significant role when it comes to investing. It can give you more control over your investments, it can increase your tolerance for risk and your ability to recover from any losses, and it can maximize your returns.

By starting early, investing wisely and giving yourself the time you need to reach your goals, you will discover the positive impact that a little bit of planning today will have on your lifestyle in the future.

I am so grateful for those of you who have read the series from start to finish. You have already put in time of learning and researching, so go forth and "Change The Speed of Wealth Creation"

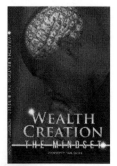
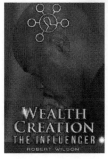